The Vision

By Thomas Matthew Roman

Dedication

To you, the person about to create and live your vision. I am just so happy for you!

Virtual high five!

-Tom

Acknowledgements

I want to thank my wife, Jessica, for her constant support and shared ideas in this book. I wanted to thank Zari Ballard for her excellent job editing and encouraging me through this process. Also, I wanted to thank my wife, daughter Riley, family, Mom, Dad, brothers, their families and close friends for making life so much fun!

*"**Matter is simply my little way of showing you exactly what you've been thinking lately.**"[i]*

– The Universe

The Universe Newsletter, Mike Dooley

Table of Contents

Dedication 3

Acknowledgements 5

Table of Contents 9

Introduction 13

Part I – What is a Vision? 17

Part II – Philosophy 51

Humility & Purpose 51

The Ultimate Attitude 55

Remove Vision Hijackers 57

Failure Isn't Failure, But Merely a Stepping Stone 69

Cash Flow Business Model 74

Grieving in the Valleys of Life 79

Successful Business is About Following Demand 81

Discovering YOUR True Wants & Desires 85

God's Universal Plan 87

How Your Vision is Transmitted to The Universe 100

Seeing the Future 117

When in Gratitude for Your Vision, You Are Wealthy! 120

Make Your Mind Your Loyal Partner 122

Going in the Direction You Are Led 124

Fusion Through Commitment 127

It is Your Responsibility to Create Your Vision 145

What is Mental Exercise & Visualization? 163

Part III: Visualization 181

Mental Exercise 186

Visualizing Greatness 198

Mirror the Millionaire Mindset with Your "Inner Coach" 215

Practice Gratitude 216

Breaking Through the Mental Barrier 230

Believe in Your Genius 232

Creating Your Unifying Principles 234

Part IV: Real-Time Vision Crystallization 239

Crystallization of Your Vision 242

Real Time Vision Crystallization Workshop 244

Creating Affirmations from Your Goals 266

Committing to Your Vision 269

Etching Your Vision into Your Subconscious, Raising Your Subconscious Vibration 270

How to Organize and Take Action on Your Goals 282

Creating Your Daily Task List 286

Conclusion 297

About the Author 300

Bibliography 301

Introduction

A clear vision does so many things to improve your life! Having a clear vision of the future you want to experience, both through the service you perform AND materially, will open up a river of flowing water from inside of you. You will become an energy releaser who feels as if you have a nuclear fusion reaction in your belly! You will go from feeling asleep, to waking up excited for the day ahead of you, before your alarm! Why are kids so excited on Christmas Eve or on their birthday? Because of the adventure of the unknown that is under the tree and in their gifts! With a clear vision, you will have this same excitement EVERY night before bed and as you get up because you will be working on and appreciating the activities and material things that you truly desire!

When you work on your top priority goal that you created, that is leading to your realized vision, your life goes from sleeping to being on FIRE!! You literally discover the fountain of youth as all opportunity in life lies ahead of you because you have a clear plan to work on your goals daily.

As you gratefully apply yourself to your highest

priority goal, you will receive inspiration. As you listen to your inspiration and take inspired action though goal setting and achievement, you will see your vision manifest. Gratitude for your current life and vision opens up the channels to pull these creative inspirations to your mind. Gratitude is harmonious relation to others and The Universe and acts as a gravitational force to pull exactly what you need to live the life you desire to you. We live in a time where the quality of life blows away that which the kings and pharos experienced. Having gratitude for all you have and your future vision puts you on the frequency of your vision and will attract the thoughts, circumstances and people you need to realize and live your vision.

String theory dictates that when a string particle vibrates it creates different particles according to its frequency. Just as a violin string vibrates at different frequencies to produce different notes, our thinking and emotional state vibrate to produce different life conditions. Want a beautiful home? Think the thoughts and feel gratitude as if you live in one. Want a new car? Think gratefully as if you have that car now. Want to be wealthy financially? Think and feel gratitude as that person now! Want to have a wonderful relationship and family? Think and feel as if you have a loving relationship and family now. Want to serve on massive scales? Think and feel gratitude as if you are serving on that level now. The key is to have your vision clearly articulated, and to have the tools to call it into your thinking with frequency, duration, vividness, intensity and gratitude.

In this book I will explain The Universal Laws of how this process works. I will walk with you on how to create the mental space on which to paint, sculpt and design your vision. I will then walk you through a simple, yet effective goal setting workshop, then show you the tools to etch your vision onto your subconscious mind so you vibrate at the frequency of your vision. Our goal with this process is to use the tool of visual motor rehearsal to get your subconscious mind vibrating at the frequency of your vision. This process of gratefully feeling as if your vision is already true, accelerates the manifestation of your vision.

I have given goal setting and vision creation workshops for years to business people, students, and many other groups. People walk in lost, sleepy and unmotivated and walk out with a laser-focused vision and with the fire of inner vision burning inside of them.

I encourage you to read this book and do the exercises in it. These are the exact tools I used in my own life and my entire vision from a few years ago is true in my daily life. As you read this book and do the exercises, you will feel like you went for a massage for your mind and soul. This may be the first time you are taking the time to think about what it is that you truly want. Please, take the time for yourself to intentionally create your future. I guarantee that you will be a different person after this book. When you are living a life that you designed, you are by-default a leader to yourself, your family and your community. The best we can do in this life is to make the most of ourselves and this book will get you started on that journey. The best we can do for others is to help them make the most of themselves, and our life-example is the best way to inspire others to do this.

Please, make the choice of taking the road less traveled. CREATE and LIVE YOUR vision today! I guarantee, when you do, you will jump out of bed eagerly enthusiastic tomorrow and each day in your future. Be prepared to live a life of adventure, laughter, fun and excitement for you and all who are in your universe. Good luck on the adventure that is your life and Godspeed!

Part I – What is a Vision?

As you may know, the 3% of people who set goals own 97% of the wealth. Please keep this in mind as you experience this book. Goals on paper are the starting point. In order to meet those goals, you need to take action, but more importantly, feel gratitude for your life as if those goals on paper have been reached and you are experiencing them in your daily life. This book will explain how to make the process of *"gratitude for your present goals"* a way of life for you. This book only relies on Universal Laws and teaches that your understanding of them and obedience to them will dictate the direction your life takes in all facets. By Universal Laws, I am explaining *proven methods* to creating abundance both in your internal world (The World Within) and in the reflection of your internal world, aka, in your life conditions (The World Without). There is more to the equation that merely writing goals on paper and taking action, however. I will try to explain it. I have found the feelings you have on the inside literally become your life on the outside. What we will do here in the pages that follow, is develop a tool kit for you to coach your emotions to be in a state commiserate with the life you truly desire on the outside. The overall experience should be exciting. Not to say that there will not be effort involved, not unlike going to the gym, but the end-result should be one that gets your blood pumping faster and your mouth salivating. This amazing range of feelings and the journey to get there, each day, is why this book was written. There is a process to achieving the life we desire and it is easier than you've been told. It all begins clarifying our desires, transforming them into goals, basically defining the life we want to live - and I will show you how to do this process. From there, you will learn to transform your goals and desires into your vision.

Your vision is the range of thoughts that occupy your thinking on a moment-by-moment basis. There are five parts to the process: 1) writing your goals and creating your vision 2) choosing to think your vision 3) feeling absolute gratitude for your vision because the thoughts that occupy your mind are your future conditions 4) listen for creative thoughts that enter your mind, apply them in your current business or learn skills to perform them 5) taking daily action on your goals in the form of best practices in business. Bob Proctor says, *"The second you make the decision (to think your vision), BINGO, you flip your brain onto a different frequency and the appropriate thoughts start rolling into your mind. That's how it works. This is one of the most important lessons I have ever learned. This is how I made millions and it will help you do the same.*"[ii] This book will provide the tools for your journey. There is no end to this process either, it becomes your very way of thinking and life. As you see your vision unfold, it is your opportunity to set new goals, to create new thoughts and to share your journey with those you want in your life. As you apply your skills of vision creation, gratitude for that vision, and daily business execution, you will be amazed, that in a very short period of time, ALL of the components of your vision will be your actual life. I know this from personal experience. This is not to say that you will not encounter challenges. It is your attitude toward those challenges that really matter. The best way I have thought to understand challenges, which will be described in depth in this book, is to even have gratitude for them. This mastery of Faith unveils the tool to know that there is a bigger, Universal Plan and that your challenges are there for many reasons. They obviously help you learn, enhance your skills, but most importantly strengthen your character, will power and ability to persevere through life's greatest valleys. Challenges are merely problems to be solved and you will be taught to experience gratitude for them as well.

Every thought in your head, moment by moment, is your vision. Your vision will become your future, your actual reality. We can create our reality or we can allow others to create it for us via the phone, web, television, movies, etc., by letting them do our thinking for us. This is our choice. You *can* learn to think the thoughts you want to experience as your life. This book will strengthen your skills in goal setting and life planning. You will put a plan in motion, scheduling time every day to work out the details of your business, and crush that plan daily! You will clarify, transform, plan, schedule, and fully *live* to your highest capabilities, all while feeling a transcendent feeling of gratitude.

The fact that you desire or want something is all you need to put it into your vision and go out there and get it. I am a big fan of keeping a decluttered living environment. There is a reality, that in a modern civilization, we need certain things. We need a car, a home, clothing, food, etc. Quoting Karen Kingston, "*It is a matter of realizing that your happiness does not depend on your ownership of things. They help you in your journey but they are not the journey itself.*" When it comes to material things and experiences, we can get whatever we want. While material things make life fun, and appreciating the service of others, especially with technology, art, music, movies, clothing, jewelry, etc., is inspiring. We don't need to clutter up our living space with them. The rule I like is that if a you no longer love a material thing or if it no longer inspires, get rid of it. Give it away or sell it. This makes the space for something you really love.

Yes, material things are fun. Starting a car you really love does put a smile on your face, but if material things really fulfilled you, then once you acquired them, then you would feel totally fulfilled. The key to realize is that material things are only a *part* of your vision. The way you are able to get the income you need to live the life of your vision is to use your skills and talents in the service of others. You never see a rich hermit. In order to make money through our goals, we must wrap them in a container called business and offer services to others. This is why every business website you see has a tab in their main navigation called, you guessed it, *"Services."* Once you realize you must serve others to make money for your material goals, your business goals become goals of service to others, your clients. This concept is completely harmonious with the Universal Law proclaimed by the

Great Carpenter from Galilee: *The greatest among us shall serve.* A part of that greatness is appreciating all of the material gifts that are at our disposal, from sunrises, to beautiful views, fine cuisine, art, fine automobiles, and any other experience or thing that we choose to include in our vision. Remember, your vision will be your future, so be very deliberate in what you choose to put in it. Then when you have your clear vision, be very meticulous in thinking of the exact vision you created as if it is already true, with gratitude in the present moment. A major part of your vision is what you are actually doing with your time, the experiences you are having. Some are purely recreational, and some are your chosen services you want to offer others. Don't feel too much pressure to exactly define these services up front as they will be unveiled to you as you think your vision. As opportunities to serve are revealed to you as you feel gratitude for your vision, take action on them and do what you can to bring them to reality quickly. The Universe likes speed and you will be surprised how quickly your vision manifests as you take inspired action.

Service is not only how we make money, but experience the true connection to The Universe. I know, personally, I feel better after a day of work that I choose to do, at my desk, or after giving a speech, then I do after watching TV all day. The reason why is that greatness comes through service to others. Service is where the real juice of life is and where you experience the highest realm of emotions. By having a clear vision, in gratitude, you will receive ideas that truly inspire you. Your inspiration will not only get you out of bed truly motivated, but affect everyone in your life inspirationally. Bringing your presently-grateful-for-your-vision, highly-motivated, high-vibration self to all the people you encounter in your life is how you continually serve throughout your day. In bringing this attitude to everyone you meet in your day, you make people want to be in communication with you. We have the opportunity to make other people's lives better from the gratitude we express to them and our continual validation and support of them and their vision. When we bring this attitude, we become a magnet for people to want to be associated with us. This likability factor is a major Universal Law in why clients stay with certain businesses. This is true in business and in all relationships. When you appreciate your significant other or children or friends, it makes them want to do more for you and appreciate you and want to spend time together.

Continually thinking your vision, but more importantly feeling gratitude for it as if it is already true, automatically creates this dynamic. You truly feel as if your vision IS your reality. The miracle of fulfillment that comes from continually realizing our vision creates not only a desire, but an innate responsibility to educate others on how they can do the same. When our life becomes an example of how to live, we naturally and intuitively show people the philosophies, skills, habits and actions that lead us to our high-vibration state. Also, it is in our self-interest to teach others how to live their vision, because when we teach someone how to do something, we are forced to master that which we teach. A part of our service is the joy received by our interaction with all with whom we come into contact. For me, service is a belief that we are instruments of a higher power to create and continue the evolution of a bigger plan. On the other side of that, is my belief that God appreciates through our senses. God appreciates all of the natural wonders of this world and those created by other human beings as well through us. Think of Yin and Yang, on one side there is service, on the other side is appreciation.

I believe that our desires and choices lead to our vision, but these desires are really a higher power inside of us pushing us to create those goals for the evolution of It's plan for progress of The Universe. This service starts as harmony and high-vibrations in ourselves; in our own home with our families and continues into outside of our homes with extended family, friends, and those we meet along the way in all walks of life, from the grocery store cashier to the human being pumping our gas into our car, to our clients. For me, right now, my service is helping people to understand Universal Laws, to assist them in having gratitude for their own vision and to give some help in engineering the business systems to actualize their vision into reality.

Earl Nightingale taught us that, *"success is the progressive realization of worthy goals."* One's self-esteem is developed in the very same way. When we work daily towards our goals, success and self-esteem naturally follow. A person who engages in activities that are low priority will always feel exhausted and empty. Watching television for hours or engaging in the jealousy-evoking interaction of social media are just two examples of low priority activities. These types of activities bring no sense or feeling of accomplishment. Working on a goal-oriented project leaves one feeling elated and full of energy. This is a high priority activity. When we work on a large project, write another book chapter, pass a test, or check off a box on our to-do list, it's an amazing feeling. When you do any of these actions, you are in the forward movement. These activities make us feel good because we are progressing toward our goals on our own time and of our own volition. We are doing what we *were put on Earth to do* and not what society tells us to do. If we listened to society, we wouldn't accomplish much. I used to say that we should see what others do and do the opposite. I have since revised that to only perform thinking and actions in harmony with Universal Laws. You have to realize that 97% of people just don't live by Universal Laws, that is why you don't do what you see everyone else doing. Society, usually led by advertising and big business, isn't meant to convey Universal Laws, it is meant to manipulate behavior to get you into financial commitments that, as we discussed above, don't lead to fulfillment. Having a daily profession to realize someone else's vision, to pay for stuff that doesn't bring fulfillment makes us soul-sick, as eloquently illustrated in the movie, *Joe Versus the Volcano*, and is not the goal of this book. We all have to work for other people for a time while in the process of turning our goals into a systematized business and gaining customers. Working for someone else is a great thing and leads to experience. It is how everyone's journey starts. When you have clear goals, think about them constantly, and put time into your day to work on them, your life transforms. I had six jobs at one time while starting my businesses and learned a tremendous amount through them, but I also had clear goals and knew the jobs were a temporary part on my journey. I was equally successful then as I am now because I had goals.

When we consciously choose our goals, work toward them daily and have gratitude for our vision, we feel fabulous and full of energy every-single-day! Arnold Schwarzenegger has a speech he gives where he encourages that we only need six hours of sleep. He says, some people say that they need eight, he recommends them to, *"Sleep Faster!"* When you are in the state of realizing someone else's vision, sleep is an escape from your life, along with other reality escaping experiences, e.g. drinking, drugs, TV & movie binges, but when you are living your own vision, somehow, your body doesn't need as much sleep. You can stay up late working on your task list and get up early the next day feeling like you had the best night's sleep of your life. This state is what I believe Mr. Schwarzenegger meant when he said to sleep faster. Mr. Schwarzenegger's life is a perfect example of this goal/vision process and, if one person can do it, so can you. That is a statement of fact. In the movie, *The Edge* with Anthony Hopkins and Alec Baldwin, there is a great scene when they choose to fight the grizzly bear that is chasing them. Anthony Hopkins says, *"Good. What one man can do, another can do. What one man can do, another can do. Say it again! What one man can do, another can do! -And again! -What one man can do... another can do!"*[iii] Remember this as you read this book and create your vision. What one person has done, you can do, too, multiplied.

There is no better feeling then to work on YOUR high priority activities – and everyone can do this! Simply schedule time in your calendar for focusing on high priority tasks and then honor this time as if you would any important appointment. If you suffered from a toothache, would get to the dentist on time? Of course, you would. Apply that same integrity to the time that you allocate for working on goals. This scheduled time can be as little as 15 minutes per day but if you dedicate yourself to this time consistently, watch what happens! You will feel full of energy, need less sleep and feel extremely motivated. You will cease to compare yourself to others. You will begin to accomplish more than you ever have in the past. Once the allotted time for a task is up, simply set the next time in your calendar for continuing action on your list and honor that time. Sticking to this simple process daily, will, overtime, allow such a cumulative amount of work to get done, you will be amazed. I notice that if I focus on my high priority tasks first thing in the morning, I am fueled for the day. Working on your goals actually GIVES you energy, while engaging in other's people's visions, takes it from you, e.g. watching TV, social media, etc. I encourage you to focus on your high priority tasks first thing in the morning, before checking email or doing client tasks, so you have your full energy to focus on them.

Too often, people over think the future and what it will take to succeed and do nothing. They become overwhelmed. The amazing truth is that we don't need to *see* far ahead to *get* far ahead. To paraphrase the wise words of Jack Canfield, "*imagine yourself behind the wheel of your car at night. To get from point A to point B – no matter how great the distance - you only need to see 30 feet ahead as shown by the headlamps.*" Driving at night, we always trust this short stretch of light to get us where we want to go. Now, apply this principle to your vision. Create time blocks - or zones - on your calendar and keep moving ahead 30 feet, one high priority task at a time. Work within these zones, giving the activity at hand 100% focus and all of your cognitive ability. Don't answer the phone, return texts, look at email or do anything that interrupts the allotted work time. If you simply *focus*, accomplishing goals is very easy. All you have to do is schedule the time and show up to do the work.

Okay, now that we have a principle for accomplishing goals, we need a process for setting them. You may say that sounds too easy, all I have to do is set time in my calendar and focus? Yes. Really, isn't that exactly how you learned your textbooks in school? A few pages at a time, then did your homework, and did it again the next day, until you mastered all of the material in the textbook? Everyone knows how to accomplish goals, but people rarely set their own goals. Setting your goals is the key to the thoughts occupying your head, aka, your vision. Goals on paper are good but it is not about *what* you write but rather what you are *thinking about* and how these thoughts make you *feel* that truly matter. You have to have the thoughts you want to think in place, think those thoughts, see those pictures, and feel gratitude as if that is THAT is the life you are living. Do the thoughts that you have now make you feel grateful? Do your thoughts make you feel excited to get out of bed in the morning? Think about this. If not, you are in the right place and if you create your goals and vision in the coming pages, I guarantee, you will open your eyes before your alarm and literally jump out of bed in the morning.

Napoleon Hill in his book, *The Master Key to Riches*, stated that the biggest tragedy of our civilization is that 97% of people do not set goals. What he meant by this is that the 97% who do not set goals never have the opportunity to share their talents with the world. Consequently, they never feel the level of self-esteem and daily motivation they as their visions were realized. Also, the greatest tragedy of people not setting goals is that the multitudes miss out on the innovations, inventions, motivation and other gifts that went to the grave with the person who never set their goals and lived their vision. *The Vision* was written to coach the reader or listener to set, think about, feel gratitude for, take action upon, to attract and achieve one's goals. When you set goals you literally create your future *in advance*. I want to emphasize this again, the goals you set, which become your vision, is the future you will experience.

In *Joseph and the Amazing Technicolor Dreamcoat,* Andrew Lloyd Webber and Tim Rice wrote, "If you think it, want it, dream it, then it's real. You are what you feel." You really *are* what you feel! Now, here is the really easy part about all of this, to shift your vibration to one of your vision, all you have to do is emotionally feel how you would feel if your vision was true. Now, as you take time to set goals and work on those of the highest priority, you will feel extraordinary. This is a fact. Creating the future in advance means exactly what it says, but you must think about your goals as if they are true and feel gratitude for them, THIS is how your vibration will match the vibration of your vision. This is in harmony with the Universal Law that we become what we think about. The fact that *your* desire created these goals is the evidence that your goals will come true. True Faith is a steadfast belief that the vision you hold in your mind will appear in the conditions of your life. Your desire, or as Bob Proctor puts it, the fact that you *want* it, is all you need to know to make the decision to add it to your vision. Wanting something is all you need, no matter where that desire comes from, if you want it, put it in your vision, then emotionally relate to your vision through gratitude, as if you already have it. This emotional relationship raises your frequency to that of your vision and makes you vibrate as if you already have it. Then as you set and achieve your goals, you actually are living your vision as your goals are met. I know, why do you have to emotionally relate to it and how do you actually do it?

Think of the concept of string theory, very basically, it says that a string's vibration can create different particles according to its frequency. Think of a violin, as its string vibrates differently, it can produce a lot of different notes. Now think of your body as a violin string, as you make it vibrate differently, you play different notes, but the notes you create are not music, they are the conditions of your life. To get on the frequency of your visualized life, you must get into gratitude for that vision as if you are living it now. You MUST ooze the wealth you desire in all facets of your life through your thinking, feeling, speech, actions and attitude. You must become that person now. This process teaches you how to 'play' your body/mind instrument. You must learn to play yourself like a violin, then learn the symphony that is your vision. Playing yourself at a frequency that will create the future conditions you desire is easier than you think, but just like learning to play the violin, will take some practice. The process of creating YOUR vision consists of constructing your goals, then creating your vision, and putting in place some very simple, yet effective tools to actually think your vision on a moment-by-moment basis and take action on the inspirations you receive. Yes, this exact process, defined in these pages, takes some time and effort, but I think living the life that you truly desire is worth it, don't you?

Our goals, our vision and our thoughts must be created

and refined. For a moment, envision a sculptor or painter. When the artist begins, his or her canvas or marble slab is a blank form. Then, the effort to create a painting or sculpture is put forth. The same process applies to constructing our vision, stroke by stroke, hammer strike by hammer strike, day by day. Our mind is a blank form upon which we paint or sculpt a vision. We must *create* it in order to bring it to life, just as Mr. Schwarzenegger recommends. Just as physical changes to our body are gradual through exercise, the same applies to developing our mental image. As you keep your vision in the forefront of your mind and feel gratitude for it, you will notice positive changes in the way you feel about yourself and in all the corresponding conditions of your life. Our vision manifests from it's clarity in mind, then through our words and actions, ultimately becoming the life that we experience.

The essence of goal setting is to crystallize the life that you want on paper. Again, only 3% of people actually ever set goals. At the beginning of my goal setting workshops, I always ask for a show of hands to see how many in the class have set goals before. Out of groups of 50, only a few people ever raise their hand, proving this statistic in my own experience. Some claim that they have goals but only in general terms. They explain that when it comes to being specific, they lose the idea. Without being clear on the specifics, life is nothing more than a generalization - a foggy vision - with no action behind it. There is no action because with no clarity there can be no plan, no specific task upon which to work in our allotted times. Goal setting is the first and most important step of the vision creation process.

Once a goal is defined, the next step is to create a mental image of this goal coming to life. In doing this, we begin to live - and most importantly, *feel* - as if our vision is already true. When Steve Chandler interviewed Arnold Schwarzenegger at the start of his acting career, Arnold stated that his intention was to become number one at the box office. When Chandler asked how he planned to do this, Arnold replied, *"I will use the same process I used in body building. What you do is create a vision of who you want to be and live into that vision as if it is already true."* Chandler made a point to add, *"Notice that Arnold said you create a vision, not wait until you receive one."*[iv] The fact that Schwarzenegger's process worked is no coincidence and we can all do it. When you point blank make other people's thoughts your thoughts through the news, politics and other channels, you receive a vision, the vision they implanted in your mind. Receiving a vision does not work! If you receive one, you won't do very much and it definitely will not inspire you, or if it does, it will be only temporary. If you have received one, look at where it is coming from and if they have your best interest in mind. I like to think of the retirement commercials when I think of this. A man or woman driving around on a motorcycle, basically wasting their best time doing absolutely NOTHING except looking at views and sipping wine. I am not saying that doing this on a weekend or on a vacation isn't a great thing, but to have that goal alone, to do nothing with your time will put you in the grave! The reason, statistically, people die after three years after retirement is they never learned the skill of goal setting and vision creation. They always had someone else create their goals and vision for them, so when they retired, they stopped having goals and their mind atrophied. A theme that we are going to think about several times in this book is the one of the gravity that creates the pressure on the Sun. The pressure on the Sun is what causes the fusion reaction of the hydrogen and helium atoms. If the gravity on the Sun somehow dissipated and removed the pressure, the Sun would immediately cease having a fusion reaction inside of it and would literally break apart and disperse into the space around it. The same is true of our body/mind when it comes to the pressure created by the goals of our vision. We need goals to keep the fusion reaction inside of us continuing to function. The fusion reaction is caused by focusing on our vision and working on our top priority tasks. This is how we continue to be energy releasers to those in our personal Universe. Without the pressure of the goals in our vision, we literally dissipate and die.

Everyone, I have ever spoken to who has taken the retirement bait has said that you can only play golf or sit on a beach for so long, then they needed to do something. Each of these people played golf, sat on a beach or watched TV, basically taking the pressure off, for a few months, then simply had to do something productive with their time. This is not the same as taking a much needed several-week vacation a few times a year to recharge. What I am saying here is that the myth taking the pressure off does not work. Again, I bring this analogy up about the Sun's relationship to gravity and the pressure required to create nuclear fusion to really emphasize it. Without the pressure it experiences, the Sun's atoms would not fuse, it would not create energy and not only it would die, so would we! Having the goal of retirement, to take the pressure off is not what we want to do! To stay in a youthful state, full of energy by the fusion reaction the pressure our goals create, we MUST set and work on bigger goals! We will talk more about the retirement myth later, but the point is, people conveying retirement as a goal to you have their own best interest in mind, the interest is on your money in their bank! I encourage you to do as Arnold did and recommends, to CREATE your own vision, and live into that vision by continually creating bigger goals and thus more pressure. When you have more pressure, you will fuse more energy inside of you and get better, faster and stronger as you live. You create such pressure by having huge goals, leading to your crystal-clear vision.

Creating your vision is exactly what this book will accomplish for you. You can set goals and create your vision to be your moment-by-moment thinking. Your vision will create a reflection, your life conditions. The key is to *feel* as if your vision is true *now*. Your thoughts and emotions are expressed clearly through your speech, so what you say is actually what you are thinking. This is where the concept of your words being a window to your thinking are 100% accurate. Your vision, therefore, is the place from which you speak, make decisions, and take powerful and focused *action*. When you truly feel gratitude as if your vision is your actual life, this is how you live into your vision as mentioned above. You become the person who already accomplished your goals. As that person, you would go for the life you actually desire and attract all of the people, skills and circumstances to bring that life into reality. As THAT person, you already are a multimillionaire and make decisions according to your wants and desires because you are certain your visualized life IS your future.

One of the main desires people list when setting goals is to become wealthy. At the end of your journey, you will find that wealth is simply a feeling of gratitude for what you currently have and for your vision. Your "richness" will come from a certainty that the people, experiences and things you really desire are on the way. The key is to feel the depth of gratitude as if you've already reached your goals and realized your vision. This is how you pull from the ether all that is needed to realize your vision. Just as the seed you plant will pull from the soil what it needs to become its full-grown potential, your vision will pull exactly what is needed to manifest. It is your choice as to what kind of seed you plant, an acorn that will grow into a mighty oak tree, or a poison ivy seed, that will grow into a poisonous weed. Both seeds pull from the soil exactly what is needed for their growth, just as you will pull exactly what is needed for your growth from the ether around you. Your vision is your seed that is cultivated through thinking of it. Gratitude for it and scheduled action ensure that it will grow into physical reality. When you feel gratitude for life, you are wealthy. Wealth is a state of mind. I believe that poverty manifests from feeling ungrateful. To complain is poverty in action. The key to manifesting wealth is simply to feel gratitude not only for what you have – which, of course, includes a life richer than the kings of England and pharos of Egypt - but also for your vision, which is certainly your future. It is the feeling of gratitude *now* that dictates your wealth, because you *already know* that your future vision will be soon realized. I encourage you to choose wealth right now, by practicing gratitude. Please read Rhonda Byrne's excellent book, "*The Magic*" for a complete course on how to practice gratitude.

In his book *Insight System for Time Management*[v], Charles Hobbes states that when a person's actions do not match up to his or her vision for the future, the result is suffering. To end suffering, we need to set goals, create a vision and take daily action on our goals. By scheduling time for high priority tasks, our suffering dissipates. A person without goals will never access the solutions that end suffering. From this missed opportunity, the suffering persists. John Lennon spoke the truth when he said that the antidote to sorrow is hard work. Working - or better yet, *serving through our goals* - is what we all should be doing with our time. When we experience difficulties or grief, working/serving alleviates the pain and if we feel good, then working/serving fulfills us even further.

There is a well-known saying that says *we either live our dreams or become a part of someone else's*. This saying is sometimes mistaken merely for working for someone else. This saying also applies to receiving a vision from the media, a political party, a religious institution, or your peer group. I encourage you to create your own vision and to live it! Most self-made people work for others for a time, and there is tremendous experience gained in working for others. The key is to be constantly thinking of and working on your own vision in your spare time and not making financial commitments based on the income from your 'job'. Invest the income from your job into your own businesses/assets and allow your business income to pay for your luxuries. This was a very hard thing for me to do, but I did it and it made all the difference.

I had a landscaping business that I ran throughout college. When I finished school, I started first startup business. Yes, there were some trials and tribulations during the first several years. There were peaks, valleys, debts to be paid and very lean times, but I kept with it. It took me around eight years to have enough passive income from my business to pay for my own apartment and all of my bills. Then, I worked on the business, travelled a lot, met my wife, got married and we bought a home together. The key to the equation is to have your businesses passive income pay for your bills. I knew it had to be passive income to achieve financial independence. A key that I hope this book communicates to you is an understanding in a larger, Universal Plan. The trials and tribulations I experienced all were meant to be as I now own 100% of my businesses and LOVE what I do every, single day. Sometimes I sit at my desk and can't believe how much I love what I do. I am blown away at the opportunity to serve in the ways my business affords me. I thank God from my knees several times per day and am truly humbled by this wonderful reality. Some of it was luck and pure blessing, and some of it was planning, but I did make the choice to live my vision and to put assets in place to pay for my luxuries. I wrote this book because I want you to experience the same thing. Also, the real amazing part of my entire journey is that I thought I was being humbled to do web development at the time. In reality, that journey created the exact situation and multiple streams of passive income that I enjoy today. I ask that you see my journey's example and know that your road, when followed with humility and gratitude to adjust your sails to the changing winds, will take you to a destination that blows away where you thought you would get to.

Using income from a job to pay for our luxuries is what is considered the *Rat Race*. Robert Kiyosaki, the author of <u>Rich Dad Poor Dad</u> describes the rate race as "*A frustrating, hard-to-break financial lifestyle, self-defeatist cycle and pointless pursuit: an employee works hard for an employer to receive a raise or a promotion and as their income increases, their expenses increase as well. As the employee's debt increases, he becomes further tied to their job and more reliant upon their paycheck.*"[vi] Don't do this. I know it is hard to delay getting the material things you want until your assets pay for them, but trust me, do it. This is not meant to put down anyone working somewhere else. Sometimes, a person's vision is as a part of a larger company, for example, some of my classmates work in the automotive industry and design cars. Their vision is a part of a bigger company, but I still recommend that people create multiple streams of income through other businesses, real estate, intellectual property, etc., so they are not totally reliant on one paycheck from one client, their boss.

Also, I know people who worked at a job, then started a business performing the service that they did at the job, then their former employer hired their new 'company' to do the service they did at their job. This allowed the new entrepreneurs to delegate certain tasks and to do an even better job than they did before, a true win/win. I know a person who is a doctor, another who is a social media specialist, and another who is a sales professional who started their own company and their old employer hired their company to do the same task they were doing at the job. It is all about the structure of simply owning your OWN business with no partners. The reason I say no partners is that having partners creates a job, not a business owner's lifestyle. Instead of creating freedom for you and your family, a partnership creates a job where each party can potentially feel as if they are doing more work than the other. If you think your partner may have complimentary skills, I would hire them as a consultant and encourage them to have their own business doing what they do, too. I had partners in my first business, and we had to split up the company. It took years to recover and put a real strain on those relationships. I encourage you that you can do this yourself and to start and own your business where you own 100%. This is the business structure you need to wrap your vision in so you can experience the independence about which we are speaking. Working toward the pursuit and realization of our *own* vision creates the freedom that is so vital to life. This freedom is the key for us to look forward to tomorrow and to getting to our desk/stage/field, etc. to perform our profession. We all have different dreams, desires, and things that we want to do in life. The exercises in this book will teach you the process to create your vision. You will learn to visualize the services about which you are passionate and then bring each one to life with structure and through gratitude.

In his book *100 Ways to Motivate Yourself,* Steve Chandler writes clearly about the visualization process: *Robert Fritz said, "It is not what a vision is, it is what a vision does." So what does your vision do? Does it give you energy? Does it make you smile? When you are tired, does it take you that extra mile? A vision should be judged by these criteria. The criteria of power and effectiveness, i.e. what does it do? What do you want to bring into being? If your vision isn't giving you energy, then pick another one. Keep at it until you develop a vision so colorful and so clear that it puts you in action just to think about it.*[vii] Our mental vision should be exciting, fun, and filled with energy and excitement. As Tony Robbins says, *"waking up and paying the lousy bills"* is not a good vision! Since our daily thoughts dictate our future, we must choose them wisely. A vision that inspires you will compel you to jump out of bed, as Mr. Schwarzenegger says, after six hours *or less* of sleep and take action! Speech is a form of that action. When you speak, your words are extremely powerful. Speak with confidence *as if* your vision has already come true. Stay in the present moment. When someone asks how you are, respond by saying *"Great!"* because, indeed, with your vision realized within your mind and soul, your life truly is great.

Our emotions should never delineate the difference between real life and our vision. If your goal is to be physically lean, then visualize yourself in the best shape possible. Eat and exercise in the manner that will get you there. If you desire monetary wealth, feel gratitude and take action. If you imagine owning a private jet, *believe* that you already do. Today, you are driving a car or taking the train because this is what you choose to do. Your jet is parked in your hanger ready to go! Remember, what you think is what you can achieve and the bigger your goals, the more service you and your organization must render.

If you visualize yourself in a tropical environment eating a fresh cornucopia of delicious foods, plan a vacation for the coming year. Calculate the cost of the trip and then set aside the *cash* money each month to make it happen. In doing this, you are living your vision in the present moment. Live in a state of *being* where the vision of your future is clear. Take daily action to realize that vision and you will *become* that person. Understand that a person *who gratefully lives as they are in the future in the present* takes very different actions than a person who lives in a state of want, lack, and ingratitude.

So, what exactly is this point of action? Simply, action is scheduling time for goals and showing up to work. It is no different from planning to exercise and getting up to do it (rather than sleeping in). Action begins the moment you sit down to work on a high priority task like writing a book (rather than watching TV). The great writer/author Ernest Hemingway set a goal to write one quality page per day.

Plan for the time to work on your goals and focus only on those with the highest priority. Our choice in taking action dictates whether our self-esteem improves or degrades. When we follow through, our integrity muscle strengthens and we feel tremendous. It is at these moments of action that we access freedom, find solutions for suffering, and move towards our vision. This is the meaning of the phrase *success is the journey, not the destination.* Each time we take action towards our goal, we personify success.

Many wonder *why there is so much suffering in the world.* Remember, 97% of people never set goals and, thus, never stop suffering. This is a very large percentage. Much of the population lives day to day focused on the past or on living a life that others have created *for them.* People are simply not aware of their thoughts, spoken words, and the power of their action. When someone speaks, inner thoughts and emotions are projected. Most people will project the past, make it their present, and define it as their future. This is how they *speak.* For example, if a person always speaks of issues from the past, these challenges continue to occur because his or her words project in the present. The spoken word has unbelievable power.

For example, people believe the wording of an advertisement as if it were true. The motivational speaker Zig Ziglar stated, *"I read the Bible every day; I read the newspaper every day. That way I keep up with both sides."* Big business - which includes the media – usually does not have your best interest in mind. Big business simply wants to sell their products. Advertising is intended to manipulate behavior, not convey truth. Tobacco companies want you to smoke, soft drink companies want you to drink big sodas, and fast food places want you to eat high caloric, unhealthy meals. Most big companies are not trying to save you or make you healthy, they just want to sell more. It is your responsibility to save yourself from harmful influences by creating and living your vision and only putting in your body and mind, food and stimuli that lead to your visualized self. We all need downtime to relax a bit and watching television is relaxing at times. If we want to improve our vibration to be in harmony with our vision, the key is that we watch programming that supports our vision. My wife calls these *Vision Shows*. There are many good movies and shows that are in harmony with what we want to accomplish, for example, *Shark Tank*. Shark Tank shows entrepreneurs pitching their business for an investor and is extremely valuable and inspiring. The hosts of the show are seasoned entrepreneurs who give sound business advice. I encourage you to only put in your mind that which you want to experience in your future. The more you put in desirable stimuli, the faster your vision will unfold. Your choice. We must think for ourselves, set goals, and take action. We must speak words and take action every day that represent our realized vision.

Part II – Philosophy

Humility & Purpose

Science teaches that we live on a revolving blue planet among billions of stars in our galaxy, among billions of galaxies in our cluster, among billions of clusters, among billions of super clusters. The universe is huge and we know very little about it. There are forces in the universe that we don't understand. Just because we don't understand those forces, doesn't mean they don't exist. They are the forces that created The Universe and keep it operating, perfectly. If we choose to think, speak and act in harmony with these Universal Forces or Laws, then our lives will unfold and develop harmoniously. Viewing life from a Universal perspective can humble us and potentially make us feel insignificant. Nothing could be further from the truth. The Universe is huge, but it took all of history to get us where we are right now, where we possess the skills to think, act, create and possess the freedom to do so. This is the point all of our ancestors worked toward, and we are the ones lucky and blessed enough to be here. The Infinite Intelligence that created us finally has the ability to create *through* us, *through* our minds, mouths and hands. In addition, this same intelligence that lives through us has the ability to appreciate through our senses as well. Look how much has been created in the past several thousand years, then, after human beings were free in the last 100 years! The things you create with your unique talents are a very important part of this continual Universal Evolution, have complete certainty of this fact.

Understand that the universe is unfolding perfectly - as *it always has* – and that you are made of the same matter as the stars. Your life and your actions are all part of this constant unfolding and development. In the grand scheme of things, your role may appear small but rest assured that it is very important. Think about the miracle of the human body. The eyes, although small in size comparison, are as vital to our body's functioning as any other part. We all can't be eyes…some of us have to be hands and feet. Think of a symphony and the variety of instruments it takes to make it sound so beautiful. We can't all be playing the bass. We must choose one instrument, focus on playing it well, and then do the best we can playing our notes so the orchestra is complete. Your role in the unfolding expansion and development of the Universe is more than vital; it was carved out specifically for you.

At this point I would like to address the power that is behind the expansion and organization of this perfect universe in which we live. The physicist and cosmologist Steven Hawking said that in order for the Solar System to develop like it did over billions of years, it has to be perfect. He said that the distance between the sun and earth is so perfect that if it were any shorter, we would burn up and if it were any farther, we would freeze. The earth has been revolving around the sun for *billions* of years. Do the math – that's pretty damn perfect.

There are forces and powers – an intelligent design - behind the creation of the Universe and physics proves this. If you are a scientific thinker, imagine this power as the sub-conscious or super-conscious mind; if you are a spiritual thinker, imagine this power as the Universal Mind, Nature, Infinite Intelligence, or The Universe; if you are a religious thinker, think of this power as God. I will speak of this power from all three perspectives throughout this book to honor the beliefs of scientific, spiritual and religious thinkers. I will also cite philosophies of all three to further illustrate the laws behind how this Universal Power works.

From this humble perspective, you realize your part in a much bigger and perfect plan...the unfolding of the universe. As Steven Hawking stated, *the perfection of the unfolding of the universe is absolute.* Earth and its inhabitants would not be here otherwise. Understanding the perfection of the unfolding of the Universe brings sanity, peace, and belief in the *Ultimate Attitude.*

The Ultimate Attitude

Wallace Waddles wrote in <u>The Science of Being Great:</u> *All is right with the world. It is perfect and advancing toward completion. I will contemplate the facts of social, political, and industrial life from this high viewpoint. Behold, it is all very good. I see all human beings, all my friends, acquaintances, neighbors, and the members of my own household in the same way. They are all good. Nothing is wrong with the universe, nothing can be wrong but my own personal attitude and, henceforth, I keep that right. My whole trust is in God.*

The Ultimate Attitude is to believe that the world - and all it contains, including the people - are perfect and in a constant state of development. The best we can do is become an active part of that development. So, how can this perfection align and coexist with the atrocities and evils of the world? Wallace Waddles explains that what seems like evil behavior in people is really a lacking of the proper development. People who do evil things obviously lack mental and/or emotional development. They may have personality disorders or mental illnesses. A seemingly normal adult with a personality disorder lacks empathy, self-esteem, and anger control. This under-development results in a person who may be abusive and hurtful. Learning to handle the stages of development in the people you meet is imperative to maintaining the Ultimate Attitude.

Remove Vision Hijackers

It is important to know how to clear the space in your mind for your vision. To do this, we must keep the ultimate attitude, while enhancing our ability to draw boundaries and take proper precautions to stay out of physical and emotional danger. There are people in all of our lives, we all have them, that are always just awesome to be around. Then, there are people whose blood type is B-Negative. They seem to always have drama in their lives and bring you into it. They could be abusers, get you in trouble, get you into a lawsuit or have some kind of blackmail over your head. The point is, even relating to them completely takes you away from thinking from your vision. I hope this next part gives you the power to love yourself enough to remove such vision hijackers from your life, no matter the cost.

I bring these next parts up about personality disorders and abuse because one of the major Universal Laws I discovered is that the best we can do to help another develop emotionally is to go no-contact at the first instance of abuse. This is in stark contrast to what you may have been taught in your life, but I will explain further below why this one step, regardless of who it is, is so important in not only maintaining your vision and high vibrational frequency, but to your self-love and personal, moment-by-moment joy. This section on going no-contact with malicious and malignant abusive personalities may be the most significant thing you ever learn, I know it was for me. The importance of this next section is beyond words and really one of the greatest gifts we can give ourselves.

A part of the Ultimate Attitude is realizing that everything in the World is in it's own perfect state of development. This includes people. Every person's emotional development is at a different place. Some people are very developed where they love themselves, then validate and encourage those in their lives through their words and actions. Some, however, are in earlier stages of development where they are learning to love themselves and may relate to others through abusive and invalidating tendencies. When you are in a romantic relationship and your significant other does something that is a deal breaker for you, what do you do? You breakup and don't talk to them anymore, right?

For a moment, put yourself in the shoes of being the person who is broken up with because you did something wrong. Your relationship with the person who broke up with you was a part of your journey. The lesson that you learned by being with them is that the certain behavior that led to your breakup is not acceptable in relationships. Hopefully, you gained the necessary knowledge on what not to do again, so your next relationship works out. If you do bring that behavior forward to your next relationship, you will continue getting broken up with until you learn. You could consider this journey of getting broken up with until you are able to relate and behave in a healthy manner in a relationship, your emotional development. Your emotional development journey was improved by the breakups because you realize what behaviors and words are emotionally healthy and lead to good relationships and which ones don't and get you broken up with. Makes sense, right?

The same holds true in any relationship we have in our lives. It is very true that you cannot change anybody. There is a saying I love, that is how can you hope to change anyone else when it is so hard to change ourselves. Think about how much effort it takes to start and keep a new habit, be it going to the gym, eating differently, getting up earlier, etc. You don't change other people, you either love them for exactly who they are or you have to make the choice as to whether you want them in your life. No one is perfect and everyone has their idiosyncrasies, but, certain people are just plain dangerous to have in your life. They can do simple things, like put you down and just make you feel bad; take all of your time, with no boundaries in business; put you in harm's way through fighting; to involving you in illegal activity that could land you in lawsuits or jail. Obviously, these are blaring red flags, but I encourage you to listen to and trust your gut and if someone makes you feel off, bad or is always drama ridden, really consider what is written next.

The best we can do for ourselves and another person's emotional development is to go no-contact with them when they perform a malicious action toward you or another human being, be it name calling, a boundary violation, or other abusive behavior. If we experience any type of abuse, we must acknowledge that this person is less developed emotionally and that they will abuse again, but next time it could be much worse where the stakes could be way higher. A small boundary crossed now, WILL yield a much bigger boundary later. Why, if you see someone call another person a name, scream at them, or worse do you go no-contact with them? Because, it is only a matter of time before that abuse is directed toward you and we should believe people the first time. When you see them relating to other people in a certain way, know that is how they relate to other humans and have the self-love to get away from such malicious people. Remember the story of *The Scorpion and the Frog*: *A scorpion, which cannot swim, asks a frog to carry it across a river on its back. The frog hesitates, afraid of being stung by the scorpion, but the scorpion argues that if it did that, they would both drown. The frog considers this argument sensible and agrees to transport the scorpion, but midway across the river the scorpion stings the frog anyway, dooming them both. The dying frog asks the scorpion why it stung despite knowing the consequence, to which the scorpion replies: "I couldn't help it. It's in my nature."* When you see someone treat another person with abuse, that is their nature. You cannot and will not change them. The only thing you can do to, not only help yourself keep your vision vibration, but to help them develop, is go no-contact with them.

Yes, we all want to help others and the best we can do to help an abusive personality develop emotionally is go no-contact with them. It is through no-contact that people truly feel the implications of their actions and have the motivation to develop emotionally. If one keeps getting dumped by significant others, perhaps it is time put the effort into developing emotionally, perhaps through reading or therapy. If one's friends stop talking to them, perhaps it is time for them to learn to relate to other human beings in an emotionally healthy, validating manner. The first time someone experiences abuse, they are a victim, the second time they are an accomplice to the abuse. This means that if you experience abuse, you get out of the relationship, friendship or business relationship because it will happen again. Emotionally developed people do not abuse others and to stay in relations to someone who is abusive is masochistic and the opposite of self-love.

You may have been taught to forgive and forget and that this is the opposite of that philosophy. Actually, it aligns perfectly with that teaching. Remember when Saint John Paul II was shot? He forgave the man who shot him. Yes, he forgave him, but the man remained in jail. Saint John Paul II wasn't having lunch with him the next day. He forgave him and went no-contact with him. Forgiveness is an inside job, meaning you are clearing the space inside of you for better emotions, which is what this book is all about. Bob Proctor says it in his book, *The Art of Living*, too. He has a whole section on forgiveness being for you on letting any bad emotions go, but, and that is a big but, you don't have to allow it to happen again, meaning, you do not have to allow the person you had to forgive to do it again.

A part of the development of this Universal Plan is helping further the development of abusive and malicious emotionally less-developed people, and as hard as it is, the only way to do this is to go no-contact with them. First, obviously, look at yourself and make sure that you are behaving in emotionally healthy ways. That you only call people by their name or a term of endearment, that you validate and encourage. By term of endearment I mean, honey, dear, sweetie, buddy, brother, etc... Then, when it comes to malicious and abusive personalities, your abrupt absence from their life allows them to feel the consequences of their abusive actions and bring the potential of better behavior into their future relationships. Again, think of when you did something in a relationship where you, yourself got dumped. That relationship was over. Let me guess, you didn't perform that same action in future relationships, right? Well, not at least if you wanted that future relationship to work. The same is true when we experience someone who is underdeveloped emotionally and chooses to maliciously and intentionally harm another human being. You believe them the first time, meaning, if they abuse once, they are an abusive personality. If they abuse, they are on the malicious and malignant abusive spectrum and are not developed enough to be in a relationship or friendship with you. The first time they abuse, you know that they are underdeveloped and that all you can do to help them develop is to go no-contact with them.

The reason I mention this part of emotional development is that all of the atrocities the World has seen were caused by emotionally underdeveloped people. If these people were removed from their relationships at the first toxic event, they never would have reached such power to cause such atrocities. If they ran a company and their customers and employees fired them and quit, they would not have gotten there. If they were in the government and their constituents and staff walked away, they would never have gotten there. No job, customer or situation warrants staying in an abusive situation. If you experience abuse, love yourself enough to get the hell out of that situation. With the clear vision you are creating in this book, you need the mental real estate they were occupying to build and house your vision.

The reason this lesson is so important is because a huge part of our own mental and emotional health is the company we keep. There is a saying that has real truth to it, *"Am I depressed or just surrounded by ***holes."* What is more accurate is to realize that if you are surrounded by abusive people, people who call names, invalidate, make fun of, use guilt, put down, to gain superiority, etc., this is a glaring sign of their emotional underdevelopment and malignant abusive nature. When you stay in any relationship like that, each time they hurt you, your vibration drops and your vision disappears because you go into survival mode. This survival mode is the fight or flight response where your vision and thoughts go to merely getting away from the toxic event you just endured. When your vision is one of survival it, by nature that we can only hold one thought in our mind at a time, is not focused on your vision, but of surviving the emotional attack. Your vibration drops to one of feeling fear where you feel hurt, angry and upset, all opposites of the vibration of wealth. This emotional hangover we experience after dealing with a boundary breaker or abuser can literally make you feel off and lose your vision for weeks after the interaction. You may have to process what happened with third parties just to get back to baseline. When you stay in a relationship with someone who abuses, you literally are saying to them that they are the superior and you are the inferior, furthering your vibration drop as, just as you are not better than anyone, no one is better than you, either. All people were created equal! Someone abuses to gain superiority over others. What made them this way? There are a lot of theories, but it doesn't really matter. Their actions are abusive and that is all you need to know. One's actions define them and dictate whether they should be in your life. Really remember, especially when you have children, that a small ouch moment, boundary broken or abuse experienced now, may result in a mind-numbing, life-altering boundary broken or horrible abuse later. When you realize the best you can do for yourself and your family is to go no-contact with malicious underdeveloped, abusive people, it changes your life. It is better to have one healthy emotional friend than a pack of friends where several are abusers. If there is a group of people you know that get together and one is an abuser, just don't go out with that group anymore and make the effort to see the individuals you want to see from that group for quality one-on-one time. Once you know someone is an abuser, just avoid them and go no-contact. A life-changing realization is to understand that there are people with whom you can spend time that are truly gifts to be with. I have friends, that when I spend time with them, it is like a therapeutic experience. Everything is positive and encouraging about the friendship. I encourage you to find and cultivate these emotionally healthy, fulfilling friendships and relationships. You do not have to spend time with people who cause emotional pain to you. This is a huge lesson to learn and one that truly changes everything. Going no-contact with malicious, underdeveloped people is a first step to your Ultimate Attitude and a powerful skill to maintaining the high emotional state necessary to keep you in the same frequency as your vision.

None of us are perfect you may say, yes, agreed, however, we learn from our mistakes and, as mentioned above, some of these mistakes cost us relationships. The mistakes we make really aren't mistakes. They are learning experiences and are actually lessons in the syllabus of life. To continue on the journey, we need only to complete each lesson. As Ben Franklin said, *"Those things that hurt, instruct."* This is true in relationships and in business. Yes, having someone go no-contact with you hurts, badly, however, the lesson learned from losing that relationship could potentially help you develop for the better and permanently improve your ability to relate to other human beings. Your ability to go no-contact with those who relate through hurtful and abusive tendencies is a huge part of keeping your vision in mind and doing the daily work you are inspired to do to realize your vision and help the World develop.

Also, one more thing about life conditions that you can't help. The previous section was to show you that you CAN control the relationships you have in your life. When you choose healthy ones, you will keep a consistent vibration and manifest your vision faster. Sometimes, you face other challenges in life, like a family member getting sick, or another challenge. During these times, it is even more important to have your goals clearly set and vision created. It is during these times that dropping the hammer, meaning, working really focused and hard on your goals is even more important. Do not let life's challenges take your vision from you, but let them fuel your vision. I encourage you to spend as much time as you can with the person who is ailing, but when you have time to yourself, work on your goals. It will take your mind off of the emotions you are experiencing. I encourage you to see these challenges with gratitude as well. To do this, you will have to trust in God's Plan, but as you do this, when the challenging period is over, you will be well on your way and closer to your vision than you ever imagined.

Failure Isn't Failure, But Merely a Stepping Stone

When one takes risks, in love or business, one encounters temporary defeat or "failure". Johan Miyanaga, in his article for the website Quora, stated, *"Every entrepreneur is a failure. You begin by failing and build your own path through trial and error. To someone who is a perfectionist and therefore trained to be traumatized by his or her own mistakes, this is a harsh reality. It requires an open mind, determination, forgiveness, and the ability to educate yourself from your own experience, not what others can teach you."* For the remainder of this book, I deem – and you may consider - the word "failure" as synonymous with the term *stepping-stone.* This will keep things in a positive perspective. Now, I did not fully understand this concept when my first business venture did not go as planned. To pay back the debts of the business, I had to let my team of nine people go and take on six jobs myself. I had two partners with me in that business and I cried at my desk at having to make the decision to move on. However, after shedding a few tears, I looked up and said, *"God, I don't know what your plan is for me, but I trust you completely"*, and proceeded to get my resume together. In the years that followed, I worked in corporate sales, as a bartender, in a shipping department packing boxes, as a security guard, worked in a garden center, ran my own company, all at the same time. In my spare time, I learned web development and started writing. I paid back all of my debts, built a full pipeline of website clients and was finally able to go full-time and focus on my current business venture.

Anthony Robbins once said that, *"When people succeed, they celebrate and when they fail, they ponder."* This was very true in my case. I made the paradigm shift by choosing to replace the word "work" in my vocabulary with the word "service", thus removing my ego from the task at hand and staying in a state of gratitude for the service I was rendering to others and the cash flow that resulted. Grateful to have my bills paid, I performed every activity in honor of something that Shakespeare once said: *Every man I meet is in some way my superior, and from that, I can learn from him.* I feel the same way today with every task I perform. With each task, no matter how humble, I can learn from it.

Here are a few of the lessons I learned from the various jobs I performed:

- **Corporate sales**: I was required to close two deals per week and, in the end, I had learned to close real business. I learned to pre-qualify, to write personal, handwritten introduction cards, to set up face-to-face meetings with qualified prospects, to do proposals and write thank you notes (or, as I like to call them, *gratitude notes*), and to close the sale. As a perk, I went on some very fun business trips!

- **Box packing**: This job required me to work the night shift, so I learned to live on much less sleep. This service also taught me humility.

- **Security**: I started writing during the downtime and met some wonderful people.

- **Bartender/Waiter**: I improved my interpersonal skills, learned some great jokes, and improved my storytelling abilities. Overall, I learned how to have good banter with people. I learned to make a variety of mixed drinks and have since applied the same creativity to cooking, juicing and making fun drinks in my own kitchen.

- **Working Retail**: I worked at a garden center where I was responsible for greeting customers and managing inventories. This taught me so much, but most importantly to really feel gratitude for those in service positions and to show them the utmost respect.

- **Running my Own Business:** By applying the skills I learned in this corporate sales position, I acquired new business for my company and sold services, starting with web development, that had high demand and a fast sales cycle.

I would have never had the privilege of these experiences if my path had not gone as exactly as it did. This variety of services not only supported me financially, each one helped to shape the person that I am today. In addition, I learned to better relate to people and to be grateful for the services provided by others. My continual development of my faith in God's plan has helped me to understand the direction of my journey and the meaning behind each individual lesson. Now, regardless of life circumstances, I understand that all paths lead to a better existence than I could ever imagine. Now, I drop to my knees, bow my head, and thank God for his plan before beginning any service that I am performing for others.

It has been said that a smooth sea never made a skillful sailor. The "failures" that I experienced were truly my greatest stepping-stones, shaping who I am today. In retrospect, think of the multitude of stepping stones you've already experienced in life and how much you've learned from each one. Imagine your life without these lessons. You just wouldn't be *you* without them. Looking back at these experiences, I am sure you smile and feel grateful for them, am I right? If that is the case, now, and in the future, as you experience these 'stepping stones', I encourage you to do all you can to feel gratitude during those times. We will discuss this more later, but just think about it for now.

Cash Flow Business Model

I have faced many peaks and valleys in business and owed a lot of money several times in my career. Because of this, I decided to never debt finance my business again. I now live below my income, using cash flow to buy equipment, pay team members, and to grow my business organically. Many people tell me that I'd grow faster if I took on more debt or acquired an investor but I have experienced both in the past and prefer not to do that ever again. As a personal decision, I choose to have a cash flow business and not a business based on valuations that require investment or debt financing. I don't need to be paying interest on a loan or have an investor breathing down my neck. I choose to run a cash flow *rich* business where true value is based on real customers, income, and profit. The alternative - where value is based on financial calculations and projections – is simply not of interest to me.

So, it is my *stepping stones* that ultimately led me to my current low pressure work environment where I save and then pay cash for new equipment and where I diligently manage my team based on the cash flow we take in. My company employs a twist on activity based costing where we pay our employees on the objectives they reach, not the actual "activities" performed. My father taught me not to confuse activity with progress and I use this axiom in each business task I delegate. I pay a fixed amount for completed work and agree to the fee with my team in advance. If the job is performed well, we keep working together. If the work does not meet expectation or if the employee is not a professional, we part ways, hopefully, amicably.

Managing in business is straightforward when you have the management tools to see what your people are doing on a daily basis. The key is to make sure that everyone is performing their tasks by their due date. This is one of the things we do at Roman Media. We organize and install automation for our clients that have a management dashboard. This is a gamechanger for a lot of clients. If one person in your company does not do their job, even for a day, your entire company can stall. The key is to be objective with people and to give them the chance to improve, but also being firm to let them go if they are just not a good fit for the job.

Another part of any business is financing it. My not taking on debt was a lesson further reinforced by Herman C. Krannert, founder of the Inland Container Corporation in

1925. Declaring that he would never take on debt to finance his business, he grew his company to 27 corrugated box plants with annual revenues of 250 million dollars and provided jobs to over 5,000 employees. Krannert was a philanthropist who endowed the Krannert School of Management at Purdue University. He started his business at 38 years old after making Vice President at his then current firm. According to Krannert, his boss said, *"I will make you vice president and put you on the board provided you always vote the way that I vote."* Since agreeing to this would compromise his integrity, Herman simply quit. Later, when he told his wife what had happened, she threw her arms around him and said, *"Great job! I am so proud of you. Now you can start your own business."* *"But we have no money for this"*, he told her. Just an hour later, to Herman's surprise, six senior managers from his former employer showed up at his door, all claiming to have heard what he'd done and followed suit, quitting the same day. They explained that they desired to start their own company and wanted Herman to be the president. When Herman explained that he had no money, the six men responded that they had combined their resources and had enough to operate for two weeks. The new company was started, never taking on any debt, and the rest is history.

I put Herman Krannert's lesson in here for two reasons. First, that you can start your business without taking on debt. Second, because you have a choice each day. He was 38 when he started his business. You have the choice to start your business now, with your existing experience and build a conglomerate, or stay where you are. Herman had NOTHING, but the experience to start the business. He had the same expenses as we all do, a mortgage, cars, insurances, food, etc., but did it anyway. Yes, he had some of his former team give him the boost he may have needed and maybe you don't have that. Let me be that boost for you. I want to encourage you to go out and start your own business and give you the confidence and faith that you, too, can have your own conglomerate. Have faith.

This lesson about debt was revealed to me through stepping-stones. Now, I own 100% of my business with no investors and no partners and I live a great quality of life. As a businessman, I work long hours managing my business but I truly love what I do and enjoy the journey with very low stress. This is the way I personally choose to live my life. If you, however, need an investment, or series of investments to live your vision, that is your choice. I sincerely realize, at the core of my soul, that no matter what challenges arise personally or within my business, things will always work out the way they are supposed to…according to God's Plan. And His Plan is so much greater than we know. The same concept applies to romantic relationships. There is a saying: *pain is a signal that you are on the wrong path.* When you feel pain in a relationship, as mentioned above, simply move on and have faith that someone who is right for you is out there. As my friend of mine says, *"They exist because you exist."* When you meet a healthy emotional person with whom you have that spark, you will know - without a shadow of a doubt - that he or she is the "one" and you will be grateful for the exact path that brought you together. It all happens according to God's Plan.

Grieving in the Valleys of Life

There are going to be valleys in life that you just can't avoid, too. There are going to be deaths, unhealthy relationships and business situations that end. During your grief in these times, I encourage you to fully grieve, shed those tears and accept that you won't be yourself for a while. In those times, try to understand and say, "*It is not my will, but Thy Will be done*" and have faith that the future will be better than the past. Even with this type of strong faith, it will take time to get through such losses, so be patient. Sometimes, time, just takes time. If you are really struggling, I encourage you to see a mental health professional who can help you through it. They call themselves mental health professionals for a reason and they can help you get back to yourself.

Grieving over situations that do not go as planned is natural, we are human beings. During these times, I encourage you to acknowledge there is a bigger plan, take the time you need to fully grieve, then, when you are ready, keep moving forward, one foot in front of the other. Move in the direction of your goals with faith and certainty that whatever awaits us will be amazing and the best is yet to come. The skills we acquire from our experiences are part of a unique education…a custom syllabus. These skills help us to serve better which, in turn, improves the conditions of life on this planet. *Failure is not failure at all.* Be grateful for your stepping-stones and be humble enough to adjust your sails to the bigger plan. Move forward in faith and have full confidence that you are working within and to help develop a Universal Plan. Vince Lombardi once said, *"It's not whether you get knocked down, it's whether you get back up."* Get back up. No matter what, get back up. Moreover, as my Mom always told me, "When things get tough, pray." Make your daily prayer anything that you want. Every day, I look up and say, *"Thank you Lord, I love and trust You"*. This simple prayer is very deep. To say *"Thank you, Lord"* shows gratitude for all the gifts God bestows upon us. *I love and trust You for Your Plan for me and for the exact experiences You put me through as I know they will result in a life better than I could ever imagine and wisdom to serve others I meet on my journey.*

Successful Business is About Following Demand

The following quote from Theodor Roosevelt is one of my favorites:

The Man in the Arena

"It is not the critic who counts; not the man who points out how the strong man stumbles, or where the doer of deeds could have done them better. The credit belongs to the man who is actually in the arena, whose face is marred by dust and sweat and blood; who strives valiantly; who errs, who comes short again and again, because there is no effort without error and shortcoming; but who does actually strive to do the deeds; who knows great enthusiasms, the great devotions; who spends himself in a worthy cause; who at the best knows in the end the triumph of high achievement, and who at the worst, if he fails, at least fails while daring greatly, so that his place shall never be with those cold and timid souls who neither know victory nor defeat."

I mean, come on, Theodore Roosevelt says it so right! When you live your vision, your soul goes from cold and timid to being on fire. You will experience this feeling as you take action toward your goals to make YOUR vision real. President Roosevelt was correct when he advised not to care at all what others think. To Roosevelt's statement, I would add that *we fail until we succeed.* Again, the reality is that there *is no failure.* If we work toward our goals, we've already succeeded and will continue to do so despite outside forces and temporary setbacks. The true genius of life, particularly entrepreneurship, is perseverance and knowing how to follow demand. The famous criminal Willie Sutton was once asked why he robbed banks, and his response was simple, eloquent, and humorous: *"Because that's where the money is."* In business, the money is where the demand is. You have to develop skills and be good at a service where there is a demand.

It took me around five years to figure out where to focus my business. It took me doing various services to figure out that there was demand for website development and other marketing services, and once I figured out where that demand was, I focused on it in lieu of everything else I was doing. I had a pesky reality that kept popping up, my monthly bills! Some early businesses I started did not produce the income as planned and I was constantly strapped financially. Once I tasted the stable cash flow my web development business generated, I focused on those services where I could get a deposit that day, get the website live in weeks, get a final payment and have other ongoing, monthly services after launch. You must persevere until you find the services that have market demand, then become the best at them! Seeing the services with demand may come to you through trial and error, a creative inspiration, or a combination of both.

My first business was a graphic design business making athletic awards. I had a few people ask about web development, said yes, we can do your website! I learned the skills and never looked back. When I realized there was demand for websites, I set a goal to become a premiere web developer and did so in six months by reading manuals, online resources and hiring a few consultants to teach me. Once you understand where the demand is, you may have to learn new skills, simply set a goal to learn the skills. Contrary to popular belief, entrepreneurship is not something you are born with, it is a skill you learn. I had a friend ask me how I got into a tech business and how I understood the technical side, I told him I just read about it and learned what I needed. I don't know everything about the web, but I learn what I need to know in order to help our clients make money through their marketing. Once you know where the demand is, learn the skills and if you want to be financially free, setup a business with recurring monthly income and services that can be delegated. A great book to read on setting up the business part is *The E-Myth Revisited* by Michael Gerber.

Discovering YOUR True Wants & Desires

The reward for perseverance is a life that you create and enjoy according to your vision. Understand that our desires are an inheritance given to us by God. This means that your desires are meant to be enjoyed by YOU. Wherever these desires originate, listen and add them to your vision. This is what makes life fun and an adventure. If you do see a marketing message of something that you want to experience, add it to your vision! If you see a trip, car, or other experience, go for it! If you want it, put it in! The material things are the easy stuff. A major goal of this book is to uncover your true desires. Your true desires are what make you fuse inside. Your true desires are what you do with your time, what you become. Ultimately, who we become is what we do with our time and talents and how we bring our unique service to the world. We want to uncover the desires that burn inside of you to be manifested through service and appreciated through your senses. If those desires are kind of foggy in you right now, have no worries! We are going to do some exercises later that will extract your true desires from you and get you a crystal-clear vision!

You manifesting your vision is a part of the perfection of The Universe. Live the ultimate attitude by knowing you are exactly where you are supposed to be. Believe that you living your vision is an important part of the unfolding of a perfect Universe. You may think that certain political and industrial situations are imperfect but this is the wrong attitude. The Ultimate Attitude assures us that these political and industrial situations are better than anarchy and, in fact, will continue to develop. It may not happen in our lifetime but we must still do our work to realize our vision today so that evolution will continue to happen. We must be grateful for our perfect life in this perfect Universe. The Ultimate Attitude knows that the time in which we live is the best time to live in the history of the world! The Ultimate Attitude knows that we live in what Earl Nightingale called "The Golden Age of Civilization" and that we all live better than the pharos and kings ever did. The Universe has been perfect so far and, therefore, we know it will continue to be perfect. This development of the Universe is all part of God's Universal Plan.

God's Universal Plan

Our ability to succeed and to move forward in the direction of our dreams and goals is directly related to the attitude with which we live our lives and see The Universe. You must learn to relate to The Universe in a way where The Universe inspires you to get to where you want to go. Think of The Universe's Plan or God's Plan, depending on your personal beliefs, as the unfolding of the universe and this unfolding is *perfect*. Seeing yourself as part of a perfect plan is the first step toward living in harmony and removing stress from your life. Trusting that you are exactly where you are supposed to be and that all of your life experiences have led you to where you are at this very moment is the *concept of true faith*. Faith is simply trust in The Universe that your vision is on its way and any experiences you have had are a part of your unique education preparing you with the tools to live your vision. To have this sort of Universal Faith is in our own self-interest as it brings peace in our life, kind of like the *Serenity Prayer*, "*God grant me the serenity to accept the things I cannot change; courage to change the things I can; and wisdom to know the difference.*" Accepting that we can't change other people and that all we can do is the best we can on our goals today is a huge bit of wisdom to realize. Again, character is forged through our experiences - both the as planned and the stepping-stones. The strongest steel is forged through the hottest flame and we are given by God only that which we can handle. In addition, we are provided the exact skills that we need at the moment we need them.

The best psychological state of mind we can possibly have is the attitude that we have done - and are doing - exactly what we are supposed to be doing on this bigger plan. The greatest gift we can give ourselves is faith. I am not speaking about a religious faith either, although that is good, too, but a faith that The Universe wants us to have our desires and that the future will be even better than the past. Thinking in this perspective is living in trust and trust is the most powerful place from which we can live.

Faith truly is evidence that The Universal Plan is perfect and that the best in life lies ahead and not behind us. This sounds so simple, but it is what is necessary to start any inspired action endeavor. To be certain that things will work out is pure unadulterated POWER. To take action as if success is the only option puts us into a state of calm serenity and present moment awareness. From this place, we have the opportunity to use all of our experiences, skills and wisdom to take powerful action each day and each moment as we perform the services for which we were born. When we are in this state, we are on fire and our life becomes an inspiration to others. When we choose to surrender ourselves and to humble ourselves to our part in this bigger plan (the *Universal* plan), the negative pressures of life simply dissolve and that space is filled with confidence and actions that attract and materialize the exact desires we hold in our minds.

If you are in a good mental and emotional state, this belief will push you to be more self-disciplined and to take further actions on your goals. If you face challenges in your life, no matter how bad a situation seems - a breakup, loss of a job or business, or even a death - this attitude gives us the gift of acceptance that these experiences are part of a bigger and perfect plan. Remember the words of 1 Peter 2:19: *This is indeed a grace, if you endure the pain of unjust suffering because you are conscious of God.* The suffering we go through in life is God's plan for us and always yields character, enlightenment and a better life than we ever thought possible.

There is a story of a prisoner of war who was captive in Hiroshima, Japan at the end of World War II. Sentenced to work deep in a coalmine, he did not understand why he had to suffer such conditions. When freedom came, he resurfaced to discover the entire city wiped out, destroyed by the atomic bomb. Right then, he knew God's plan. He would have certainly been dead if he had worked on the surface. By having to suffer in the coalmine, his life had been spared. With gratitude for God's Plan, this man went on to live an extraordinary life. If a situation makes you uncomfortable, simply say, *"I appreciate the feelings and conditions I have now, God, because they are the stepping stones for skills developed on your path for me. You are stretching me to become better so I will have the skills necessary when I need them. Thank you, Lord, for stretching my comfort zone."*

When you are in the comfort zone expanding state, when you take a big risk and you find yourself overwhelmed with anxiety, where you may lose sleep and have the situation on your mind, immediately, think of the adventure of your life and your new skills being developed. Get into a state of power around the comfort zone shattering and know, with 100% faith and certainty, that you taking this risk, or going through this experience, is going develop skills, talents and a reservoir of strength that would not have developed without what you are going through. Have complete faith in this and when that anxiety feeling surfaces, embrace it and generate power from it.

Think of the Sun. The massive pressure it is under is what causes the hydrogen and helium atoms to fuse, releasing tremendous energy. Think of the pressure you are going through as making you *'fuse'* within and release energy from the pressure to become stronger and more powerful from it. Think of yourself as an athlete going into a championship game. You have to play the game in order to win. This comfort zone expanding anxiety is natural to any athlete playing any big game. Consider the pressure you are under as a blessing and know that God creates the strongest people by putting them through experiences that produce such pressure. If the sun didn't have the pressure it has, it would not produce the light and heat it does. If you weren't put through circumstances with pressure, you never would develop. If you are not feeling pressure, your thinking and goals aren't big enough! Through these experiences your greatest talents and skills are developed. As Horace says, *"Adversity has the effect of eliciting talents, which in prosperous circumstances would have lain dormant."* Without pressure and challenges, you simply would not be growing. Welcome these feelings and when you feel that pressure, let it fuse inside of you and release the same pure, Universal, unfiltered power as nuclear fusion in a star. Remember, you are made of the exact same substance as a star, just let the pressure you are under fuse into power!

Have faith that your comfort zone expanding experiences are for your best life possible. This belief that the best is now and *yet to come* is the hallmark of The Ultimate Attitude – but this takes practice to attain. Understanding that we are exactly where we should be is a revelation that relieves the pressures on the human mind. As hard as life may seem, our ability to trust in God and His divine plan leads us to a greater life. This amazing psychology holds the key to powerful thinking and, ultimately, our happiness. If we understand that all redirection in life is for the best possible outcome, there is no fear. Have faith that your life path is a unique education. All you need to do is focus on your vision and do today's work to the best of your ability. Your gratitude in the perfection of a Universal Plan, and your important part of it, will give you the skills necessary to perform future service and to traverse any stepping-stones that lie ahead.

Remember that successful people are not without challenges but rather they have learned to seek solutions and solve their problems. I speak of such challenges because I went through many of them on my journey and each taught me a lesson I needed later on. Each experience of your life is unique to you and the skills you develop are your education. Think of all of the unique experiences of your life and the education you received. Even if there was suffering, the situation led to the best possible outcome. This is how life works and it is truly amazing. This is why we often refer to bad situations as "blessings in disguise". Challenges we face now and those yet to come happen for a reason and we can accept the outcome with joy, humility, and gratitude. When one faucet stops, another opens up and starts flowing. When one door closes, another will open. If we pay attention, we will see and recognize all opportunity. This is true in business, our relationships, health, finances, and all facets of our life.

Be certain that God has a plan. If you feel regretful, simply humble yourself and say, *"Thank You Lord for having that situation transpire exactly as it did. Please give me the strength to see and be grateful for your plan. I accept the circumstances of my life and am grateful for the skills and lessons I learned during these experiences."* This prayer expresses confidence that God's plan is greater than we know. Each outcome will be brighter and more colorful than the one before. The act of prayer helps us to "deal with" the past by showing us now that the decisions we made were correct! We are exactly where we are supposed to be, did exactly what we were supposed to do and dealt with people exactly as we were supposed to at the time with the awareness we had at that moment. This process of understanding and clearing out the past *makes room for your vision.*

I love the Autobiography of Benjamin Franklin and have read and listened to it several times in my life. One time, when in the middle of reading it, I had a dream that I was in Philadelphia, standing in a room of an old historic building. This building had single-pane windows – the kind where the bottom of the glass is thicker than the top due to settling over time. As I stood in that room, a secret door popped opened to reveal Benjamin Franklin sitting at a desk. He said to me, *"Tom, I've been waiting for you"* to which I replied, *"Ben, where have you been? Why haven't you come back sooner?"* He said, *"Tom, you see, as a human, you have no idea what the Universe is. When you leave the physical world, you can go anywhere in the universe with the blink of an eye. Don't mourn those who leave your world as they are experiencing a life you can't imagine."* Paul McCartney wrote *Let It Be* and *Yesterday* after dreaming, the Old Testament of the Bible is full of dreams and it has been said that God speaks to us in dreams, and I believe this dream had some truth to it.

This dream made me realize that I know so little about our World and Universe. It helped me see that when I fight against my faith and trust in The Universe, doubting the perfection of my life, I rob myself of happiness in the present moment. When I fear the unknown or have regrets about the past, I am robbing myself of joy. When I allow this doubt and fear to creep in, I am showing ingratitude to God and the Universal Plan. Alternately, when I live in a state of surrender, no matter what is going on in my life or business, my thoughts lead me to peace, serenity and joy. By surrender, I mean that I see myself as an instrument of God…as his hands and feet. My words are His words and I am certain that all experiences will lead me to a colorful and beautiful outcome. God gives the birds enough to eat each day, right? They do not fall out of the sky from starvation. Thus, you will be provided for as well. All you need to do is feel gratitude for your vision and take action toward your goals. Remember, all you need to see is 30 feet ahead to get to where you want to be. Be confident and grateful right now that you are en-route to your destination.

One idea we are really going to explore in the goal setting workshop is to establish our true desires and to separate them from borrowed desire. The word "desire" (de-sire) comes from the Latin meaning "Of the sire" or "Of the Father". One of the major goals of this book is to help you clarify your true wants and desires. I believe there are two types of desire, desires of service and desires of appreciation. The Universal Law that the greatest among us shall serve is as true now as it ever was. Once we get clear on our vision, the ideas of service propagate into our minds to create a life reflection of our vision. Bob Proctor says that all we need to know is that we want something in order to know of its future existence in our life. You don't need anyone's permission either. If you truly want something, visualize it as a part of your life with gratitude, listen for inspiration, perform inspired action, then go out there and get it.

So, if desires are given to us from 'The Father' or from 'The Universe', depending on your beliefs, then all we need to do is be careful that our thoughts reflect our desires. Thinking about that which we desire is what our conscious mind was intended to do. One might then wonder how it is possible for God's Plan and free will to co-exist. God, indeed, gave us free will to make us accountable for our words and actions. He may impel us with desire but we alone are accountable for our conscious mind, mental health and thinking. It is up to us, individually, to think about that which we desire and to show ownership and gratitude for our vision. Through the gift of free will and thought, we can impress upon The Higher Power whatever we choose. This power is objective and gives us exactly what we convey through our thinking. We will receive ideas to manifest exactly what we think about, even if painful, because these are the thought images we are impressing on our mind and thus, Universal Mind. It is up to us to convey the vision we created by thinking it and, most importantly, to feel gratitude for it. Gratitude is harmonious relation by focusing on the best we have, and thus brings more of the best. Gratitude opens up a wider channel of communication with The Universe and accelerates inspiration. Our mind's vision is *the seed* and a gravitational force inside of us. This is the same gravitational force that makes plants grow. The thoughts we have, just as the seed pulls from the soil what it needs to grow into the type of seed it is, will pull from the ether exactly what is needed to grow the vision we hold in our mind. Our vision seed will germinate our minds with the inspirations of service and action on those ideas will lead to corresponding life conditions of a realized vision.

Dr. Martin Luther King, Jr. wisely referred to this process as "stepping up the staircase". Of course, the exact opposite is true if we hold thoughts of lack or if we dwell in the pain of the past. This would indicate taking a step *down* the staircase. The Universe will give us inspiration to get exactly what we think, so it is your choice as to whether you want to walk up or down the staircase by the thoughts you hold in your mind. To consciously feed your mind thoughts that take you down the staircase is to intentionally hurt yourself, SO CHOOSE NOT TO DO THAT. To allow borrowed thoughts and desires to fill your mind will only take you closer to the exact bad emotions they elicit. It has been my observation that much of the thinking conveyed to us is destructive because as we step down the staircase, we need outside help. Much of current industry only exists to serve dysfunction. When you step up the staircase, you will become self-reliant. As you hold a carefully crafted vision, you will see why your thinking will be pretty much be the diametric opposite of what you see in the mainstream. Those thoughts that make you feel bad simply are sending a vision that says you want to feel bad to The Universe. You will get exactly what you think according to Universal Laws. Think the thoughts of the future you want to experience so you can have more, do more and be more. The exercises in this book will teach you to walk *up* the staircase, one glorious step at a time. Believe, feel, and live in the Ultimate Attitude. Know in your heart that you are exactly where you are supposed to be and that the future will be EXACTLY the thoughts you hold in your mind. You may say, *"Come on, really? How does this work?"* This next section is a little technical, but please trust me, as you grasp the concept, it will be like a mind grenade that shows you exactly how visualization works and how your vision is transmitted to The Universe.

How Your Vision is Transmitted to The Universe

The book <u>Flatland: A Romance of Many Dimensions</u>[viii], written by Edwin Abbott, illustrates the relationship between our vision and how a higher power sees our thoughts and gives us inspiration to create those thoughts. In this book Abbott describes a world that resides on a two-dimensional plane. This two-dimensional plane may be considered the top of water where the water meets the air, or the top of a table. There are many two-dimensional shapes of beings in this flat plane. There are circles, pentagons, triangles, squares, etc. These figures can only move right or left in their world and they can only see each other as lines. Think about it for a moment. If you put four pencils in the shape of a square on a table and looked at them from several angles with your eye at the side of the table, all you would see are lines of varying length. Better yet, think of putting a coin on a table top, then bringing your eye to the side of the table, all you would see is a line the length of the diameter of the circle, right? The same holds true for any shape, including triangles, polygons and circles. If, however, you raised your perspective to view that shape from directly above it, you would see the shape, for example, a square and whatever was inside of that square. Please, let's take a moment to look at different dimensions and how the higher dimension could potentially see the thoughts of the lower dimension and project ideas back to them.

Let's start with the zeroth dimension. The zeroth dimension consists of a point in space that is infinitely small and content in and of itself. It has one endpoint and can see nothing except itself. In order for that point to see into the first dimension, it has to look in a direction that it never has before, which is opposite to itself. Just bear with me here, this will come together in a moment. If we trace the shape that being makes as it looks opposite to itself, we will discover that the shape it creates is a first-dimensional line. The line has two endpoints.

Pretend that a one-dimensional world was just one long line, line land, and on this line lived many smaller lines. Some lines are long, while others are short. If these lines resided on a longer line, they could only have two neighbors, one to their right, and one to their left. Picture a line having two eyeballs, one on each end point and picture the brain of that line to reside in the middle of the line and between the eyes. If that line looked in the direction of another line, all it would see is a point.

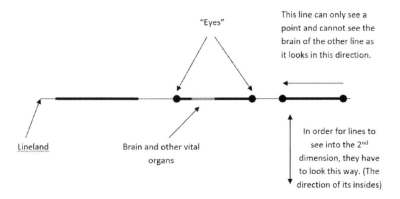

"Eyes"

This line can only see a point and cannot see the brain of the other line as it looks in this direction.

Lineland

Brain and other vital organs

In order for lines to see into the 2nd dimension, they have to look this way. (The direction of its insides)

To examine this, put a pencil on a table and look at it pointing at you. What do you see? You see just the point, basically a dot, and not the inside of the pencil. So, the only thing that one-dimensional lines ever see in their entire life are points. When they look at these points, they cannot see past them, so they cannot see the brain or other vital organs of another line. Okay, again, please bear with me here. Now in order for this line to see the second dimension, it must look in a direction opposite than it has ever seen, just as the 0th dimension did. The one-dimensional being has to look in the direction opposite of its insides in order to see the second dimension. When we trace the direction of that first-degree line looking in the opposite direction than it has ever seen before, the shape that line makes is that of a square.

This square has four endpoints and lives in that two-dimensional plane, e.g. a table top, that we discussed just a moment ago. The only things that the two-dimensional beings can see are lines, regardless of the shape of the object at which it is looking. Again, think of bringing your eye to the table top and looking at a coin at its side, you will only see a line the length of which is equal to the diameter of the coin. The same is true if you were looking at a square, triangle or polygon from its side, you would only see a line the length of its cross section.

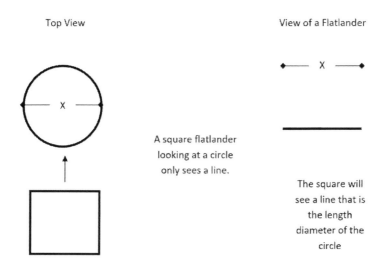

Top View

View of a Flatlander

A square flatlander looking at a circle only sees a line.

The square will see a line that is the length diameter of the circle

Now, picture a square looking at a line on the line-land we discussed above. If a square were to look at a one-dimensional line it could actually see the brain of a line. If that lines thoughts were pictures that were projected onto its brain, the square could theoretically see the thoughts of the line and project new thoughts onto the line's brain.

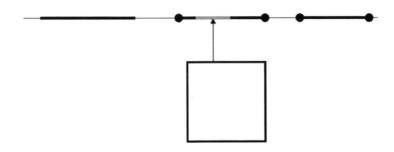

Okay, now, back to the two-dimensional plane, the table top. Now pretend that the brain and other vital organs of the square reside inside the square. Pretend that the square has a round blue circle as its brain. All other Flatland, two-dimensional beings could see is the lines that surround that square, just as if we were to look at it from the side of the tabletop. So, if a circle looked in the direction of the square, all it would see is a line and not its brain.

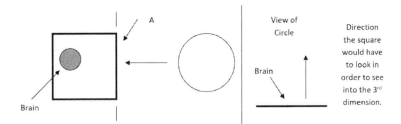

If this second dimensional being wanted to see into the third dimension, it would have to look in a direction that it has never looked before, which is the direction opposite to its insides, or opposite to its brain, which would be straight up, perpendicular to the tabletop. If we traced the square going into the third dimension, the resulting object would be a three-dimensional cube with eight end points.

If a three-dimensional cube were to look down on a two-dimensional being, think of looking down on the tabletop, the three-dimensional cube could actually see the round-blue-brain of the two-dimensional square about which we just spoke. Now just pretend that the two-dimensional being's thoughts were projected on its brain by pictures. If this were the case, the third-dimensional being could actually see the thoughts and dreams, aka, The Vision, of the second dimensional being. Then, the third dimensional being could project thoughts onto the brain of the second dimensional being in the form of inspiration. Think of projecting these thoughts as drawing something on a piece of paper or pointing a projector's image onto the table top. Think of seeing the thoughts of the two-dimensional-square, then drawing or projecting ideas on how the square could accomplish its vision.

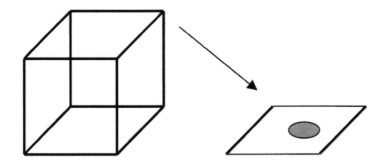

Now back to our example. Let's now pretend that the three-dimensional cube's brain and other vital organs are inside of it and let's say that the three-dimensional cube was looked at straight on by a three-dimensional sphere. The three-dimensional sphere would only see a two-dimensional square, and not the cube's brain. Just as if you look at another human being, you can only see their face; not the inside of their head, e.g. their brain. Now in order for the third-dimensional being to see into the next dimension it would have to look into the direction opposite of its insides, or opposite of its brain.

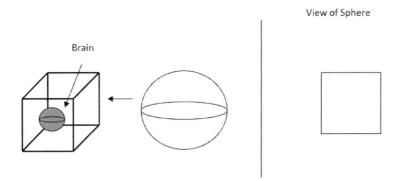

Brain

View of Sphere

The following diagram represents dimensions, the shape of an object in that dimension, the number of endpoints of that object, what they would see in their world and the direction that they would have to look in order to see the next dimension. Let us study the following logical diagram.

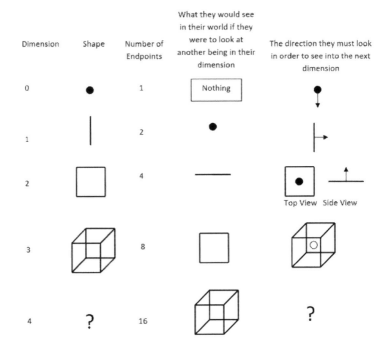

As we can see the number of endpoints that each figure creates as it goes into the next dimension doubles. So the fourth dimensional being that will be created when we trace the lines as the third dimensional being looks opposite to its insides will have 16 endpoints. We don't know what a fourth-dimensional being looks like because we can only see in three dimensions.

Imagine this now, a fourth dimensional being is able to see the brain of the three dimensional being, just as the beings of the higher dimension were able to see the brains of the dimension below them.

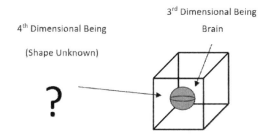

And if we, the three-dimensional beings, project our thoughts in images, then the higher dimensional being can see our thoughts and project new pictures on our mind in the form of new ideas. So, the direction of our insides is the direction of our brain, which is the direction of our thoughts. You may say that this seems ridiculous. But think about it for a moment. When you pray, do you speak? Usually not, however God hears you. When you pray you are thinking and projecting images onto your brain, God sees these images and answers your prayers.

This realm of the fourth dimension is similar to the principles about which Plato spoke in his theory of the forms. Plato described the forms as *"Abstract entities that exist independently of the sensible world. Ordinary objects are imperfect and changeable, but they faintly copy the perfect and immutable Forms.*" This basically means that our whole world is an imperfect copy of another world that is hidden from our view. This has also been spoken of in the Bible in John, Chapter 7, Verse 38, when Jesus said: *"Out of his belly shall flow rivers of flowing water."* I believe that the forms, the flowing water from our bellies, the fourth dimension are our World Within. We consciously create our World Within by the vision that we keep in our mind. The thoughts you have in your mind, right now, are being communicated to a higher power and inspiration on how to accomplish those ideas are being brought back to you. The thoughts we have in our mind stimulate inspiration to accomplish those thoughts. If we think great thoughts, of a future that is magnificent, we will be given inspiration to accomplish those thoughts. If we think thoughts that are sad, for which we are ungrateful and that we complain about, we will be given thoughts to manifest sadness, ingratitude and painful conditions. This process is objective and will give us whatever we want. We show The Universe what we want through the images we hold in our mind.

This is a way to conceptualize how and where creative thought comes from and how we harmoniously pull from the Mind of God thoughts to bring our vision to reality. New ideas come from this next dimension of thought and are given to us in perfect harmony with the thoughts we hold in our mind. You can make the decision now to either hold a vision in your mind that you create, a vision that you love, or to pursue thoughts that others implant for you that make you feel bad and about which you complain. Remember that Benjamin Franklin conceived God to be the fountain of wisdom, he thought it right and necessary to solicit his assistance in obtaining it. Think about what Benjamin Franklin is saying. Ben Franklin obviously held a powerful vision and was given inspiration that led to amazing results.

When you creatively visualize yourself and your dreams, you are communicating your deepest desires to another dimension, consider it the Deity, God, the Fourth Dimension, Universal Mind or whatever, but you are speaking in the language of the universe, the language of pictures, dreams, visions and gratitude. These pictures we hold in mind, when clearly identified and revisited with great frequency, are the source of our prayers, our innermost desires and what we want to accomplish and experience in our lives. It is in your own best interest to fill your mind with thoughts you want to appear in your life.

When people realize the relationship of their thoughts to The Universe and that their thoughts are their future, they will see the truth in the statement excerpted from The Power of Focus[ix], *"If you realized how powerful your thoughts are, you would never think a negative thought."* Remember what Paulo Coelho said in The Alchemist, *"Dreams are the language of God. The language of the soul is one that only you can understand."* You are truly the only one who knows the content of your mind. I encourage you to think thoughts you want to experience in your future through a carefully crafted vision.

Let's look at another example of how The Universe gives the gift of creative thought in response to the vision we hold in mind. Let's think of our two-dimensional Flatland again. Let's pretend that there is a square safe that contains a rare gem. In Flatland there is a circle next to it that wants to get that gem, but it can't because it is behind a line and the circle cannot penetrate the line. A third-dimensional being could not dip into the second dimension, pick up that gem up into the third dimension and place it back into the second at a different location, that would break the laws of the two-dimensional universe.

 | View of the Circle

What the third-dimensional being could do, however, would be to see the desire for that gem on the mind of the two-dimensional being, then through the opportunities that exist in the two-dimensional universe that would further its plan, project an idea on the two-dimensional being's mind where he or she could serve others and earn enough money to buy the gem from its owner.

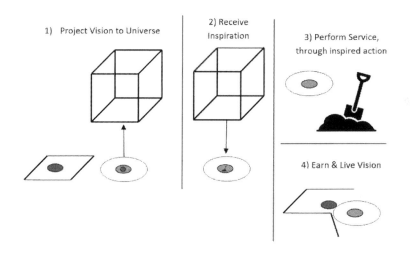

1) Project Vision to Universe

2) Receive Inspiration

3) Perform Service, through inspired action

4) Earn & Live Vision

So the process would go like this, project your vision to The Universe through thinking and gratitude for your vision. The Universe has a plan and has jobs and tasks that will further the development of Its plan. The Universe wants to give ideas to manifest one's vision to someone who is grateful, because gratitude is a gravitational force to wanting to give more to you, where ingratitude and complaining are repulsive opposing forces and pushes people and The Universe away. Gratitude is how we harmoniously relate to The Universe and how we are given ideas to realize our visions. We will speak about gratitude more later in this book. The Universe then projects an idea onto the mind of the person projecting the vision. Ideas for The Universe's various jobs may surface to other people, too, so it is important to act quickly on the inspiration when given.

Think of it like this, think of a city, for example, New York City, and how quickly it is being developed. It is going to develop and move forward no matter what, just like The Universe is going to continue to develop. As you gratefully think your vision, you have the inspired idea to build a foundation for a building in a different, more efficient way. That idea popped into your head and will pop into someone else's head, too, who is thinking their vision.

New York City is continuing to develop and that new idea will eventually be used by someone, but the question is will you be the one who sets a goal and takes action to implement it? The Universal Plan develops the same way, in many facets, with many different 'jobs' or 'tasks' that have to get done to further its evolution. As an inspired idea enters your mind as you think your vision, I encourage you to act fast and get the ideas started and work on bringing your ideas to others through service. When an inspiration is used to serve others, it yields the remuneration that earns the vision originally projected. Said another way, when inspired action is taken through service, the resources necessary to earn and live your vision are manifested.

Sounds pretty amazing, right? Think about what comes to you in the shower, ideas? Thoughts and ideas can come to you anywhere, especially in the shower, a closed box with four walls! They can pop in and out of our dimension and into our minds. As we hold our vision in mind and be grateful for our vision, these ideas will come to us, all we have to do is capture them and take action! Les Hewitt, Mark Victor Hansen and Jack Canfield in their book, The Power of Focus, give the statement, *"Did you ever have a big idea in the middle of the night? You sit straight up in bed and your mind is racing. Usually, you only have a few seconds to capture that idea before you lose it, or your body says, "Go back to sleep, it's three o'clock in the morning!" In fact, you may drift back to sleep, wake up hours later and have completely forgotten what your great idea was."[x]*

We all have had this happen. As you are holding your vision in mind with gratitude, this will happen to you all the time! Make sure that you record your ideas and do something about them! The way to make them real is through action, which we will discuss in later. It is our responsibility to act on the gift of creative thoughts. Creative thought is the greatest miracle of them all and you taking action on them is what will make your vision reality. Thoughts are gifts and can go through the walls with brilliant clarity and leave with the same quickness unless you do something to capture them. Now that you see the power of your mind and how it communicates with The Universal Mind, take the time later in this book to clarify your vision. Then focus your mind and physical energy to bring your creative visualizations to reality.

Seeing the Future

There are those who can see the future. No, these people are not mystical or clairvoyant. You, too, can see the future simply by holding gratitude for the vision of your goals in the present moment. The future is an act of our creation. Your future can be whatever you want it to be. To make it happen, you simply transfer your vision to the Universe through your thoughts. Your vision is your order, like placing an order in line at a fast food restaurant. The concept of mental ownership means that you *feel* in mind and soul as if your vision is already true. Your body and sub-conscious mind cannot tell the difference between a thought and reality. This means that you must vividly *see* your vision and *feel* gratitude for the life that you desire in the present moment. To see the future is to take mental ownership of your vision and vibrate as the person living that life right now. When you take action from the place of your vision being true, you take bigger risks and you attract into your life the material means required for your vision. The reality is that these are not risks at all because with gratitude for your vision and action on your inspiration, you will attract all of the material means your vision needs to flourish.

Often, as children, we are told to *think before we speak* lest we say something inappropriate. As adults, we now know that there is more to this saying than meets the eye. Our words are very powerful. Whenever you are thinking and speaking, examine your thoughts and speech carefully as they will dictate your future. Ask yourself, *"Do the words that come out of my mouth represent the future that I want to have?"* Understand that the thoughts you think and the words that follow dictate your future conditions and experiences. In reality, your thoughts equal your goals and when you turn these thoughts into words and then into action, you have created your future. If you hear a story on television that makes you feel bad and then repeat that story to someone, you are perpetuating the bad feelings associated with that story, instead of perpetuating gratitude. In each moment, choose to only use your vocal chords to create sounds that illicit feelings in you and those to whom you are speaking that promote the future you want to have. You can choose to discuss things that make you feel bad, or things that make you feel great. One will bring more undesirable situations in your life, while the other will bring desirable situations in your life. It is your choice; every-single-time you speak! Choose your thoughts and words wisely as they WILL become your future.

That well-known, age-old adage *we become what we think about* is very accurate. The same is true about the famous phrase, "*I think, therefore I am*". You *are* the thoughts that you think and so will be your life. Your thoughts are your vibration, your very frequency in The Universe. There is a reason that these sayings have been around for centuries. The wise before us knew this. Our speech is a window to our thinking and our life conditions are a reflection of our thinking. This is true not only in the spiritual world but in the physical world as well. In the physical world, our thoughts become our speech; our speech leads to our actions and amplifies our thinking through our communication and leadership abilities. Our ability to communicate can bring power to us and to those we associate with or it can take the power away. Our thoughts, words and especially our actions ultimately define us and determine our life conditions. Decisive speech and clear, organized thinking and action will yield a clear, organized life. Messy, disorganized thinking and action yields a messy, disorganized life. It's really that simple. This is not positive thinking versus negative thinking. It is a matter of knowing that your thinking equals your future. It is your choice whether that future will be the vision you created, or disorder, chaos and dysfunction.

When in Gratitude for Your Vision, You Are Wealthy!

I tell you this next section from experience. As I mentioned, my entire vision board from a few years ago is 100% realized. I keep re-creating it with new goals. The reason I speak of this with such authority is because I experienced it personally! There are two methods of thought and both are reflected in how people respond to the question *"How are you?"* The vison-creator always answers *"Great!"* because no matter what, this person is in gratitude for their vision because they know that their vision is their future. When they speak, it is if their vision is already true, and that life really is great! This person wakes up each day with a clear vision and ready to begin a high priority task. He or she is eager to move down their list until each task is complete. The vision-creator is excited about life because he or she lives in the present moment as if their vision is already true and attracts what is needed to live that vision. Now, the non-vision-creator always responds to the same question with *"Well, could be better"* or *"Please, don't ask!"* or *"Do you really want to know?"* The non-vision-creator's future will be exactly what their past was because they are not actively creating it. If their past was a struggle, they speak in terms of their life being a struggle, and guess what, their future is exactly what comes out of their mouth, more struggle. This is hell on Earth and why it has been said that, *"Where there is no vision, the people perish."* The road they see 30 feet ahead of them is the same as the road 30-feet behind them and their lack of a vision, or their borrowed vision, keep them perpetuating in this hell on Earth. By focusing on our vision as we think, we can visualize ourselves and feel gratitude in that reality, then take action on our goals to make it reality in the physical world.

Statistics show that 3% of people live with the first attitude and 97% live with the second. Obviously, it is this same 3% who own most of the world's wealth because these are the people who invent new things, raise great families, run successful businesses and strive to move society forward. This three percent are the self-actualizers. Self-actualizers construct their visions with the power of their minds, receiving their inspiration to create through daily work or service.

Make Your Mind Your Loyal Partner

Dr. King said, "*Faith is taking the first step even when you don't see the whole staircase.*" Your thoughts and actions are the steps on your staircase and you can go up or down - it is completely your choice. First, you have to be clear on what you want. I hope this book helps you get perfectly clear on what you want. Once you are clear on your vision, it is up to you to think thoughts and speak words that put you in mental ownership of your vision. Then, number your goals in order of importance and get to work on the first one. It is that simple. Our thoughts and words have powerful resonance in the Universe and bring to us exactly that which we think and speak. Thoughts are things and words are just SO powerful! Learn to focus your thinking to increase your emotional vibration, only thinking about your goals and your vision, and then take the action to get you there. When you are clear on your goals and work on them daily, you feel amazing throughout the day and energy is released. Realize that your mind can be your closest ally or your worst enemy. The time to make it your ally is upon you, here and now. Your mind can easily become your worst enemy when you do not consciously construct the thoughts that you think. At first, the process is like wrestling a bull but, with some practice, your mind will become your loyal partner.

Going in the Direction You Are Led

The courses you took, major that you studied in school, or jobs that you had does not have to dictate your vision choice either. Like my friend says, "40 is the new 18". You can choose to pursue your vision at any time! While you may get a faster start starting a business in an industry you know, doing something that truly inspires you is totally within your grasp. I have a friend who chose to start acting in his late 30s, now, he is a regular actor and has been in most television shows and many A films. I studied Mechanical Engineering in college, but my inspirations led me in another direction. I tried a few different businesses, but found demand in website development. Now, my company manages thousands of clients and has a growing team with a great reputation in the marketplace. I teach business website development at local colleges and feel privileged to use my experience to help people generate leads and automate their marketing and sales. I thank God that I never had a plan B or safety net. If I had, I would have been robbed of this amazing journey. My life is exactly as it should be. The reason I tell you this is that I want to instill in you that your life is exactly as it is supposed to be, too, and to encourage you to keep persevering. Keep putting one foot in front of the other and perform your next goal to the best of your ability.

As you work on your goals, remember, your actions surely follow your thoughts, speech, and feelings. When you think and feel grateful for your vision, schedule time and take action on your goals, you live in a state of pure power and flow. You automatically feel incredible about your life and the world around you. This is a state of infinite possibility where you become a juggernaut that can't be stopped. As you accomplish your goals, you are going to feel and be unstoppable!

Ask a hundred people what their vision is or what they want their life to be and ninety-seven of them will look at you confused, stating that setting goals just isn't for them. These people cannot see the future. As Dave Ramsey says, *"Ignorance of the law is no excuse for breaking the law."* In my Vision Creation Seminars, I've seen people walk in completely lost and walk out on fire. They leave the seminar with an inner vision burning in their eyes. They simply needed to get clear on their goals and set a plan to achieve them. They needed to understand the process to create their vision and make gratitude for that vision their emotional norm. It takes just minutes a day to get on the frequency of your vision, then time in your calendar to work on goals that ensure your vision becomes realized.

Hold a clear vision and work every day on goals to accomplishing that vision, without a safety net or plan B. When you put yourself in a position where you must succeed or you do not eat… watch out world!

Fusion Through Commitment

If you want to succeed massively, this chapter is for you. I am talking on levels never seen before. I am talking to serve on a level that puts you at the top of your chosen field, the current muster roll of civilization. This is totally possible and if being the best at what you do is your goal, then you will want to really listen to this part. We have discussed several times the concept of having a nuclear fusion reactor in your belly by creating enough pressure to cause fusion in yourself. I really want to explain this here in this section.

Think of the concept of what a star is. A star is a huge volume of gas, starting as hydrogen, that collect together in space. The gas' volume is so much that it causes such massive gravitational force to be applied to it, that the pressure on the hydrogen gas atoms actually produce a reaction called fusion. The fused hydrogen atoms then create helium and they, too fuse and the process continues. When an atom is split, it causes nuclear fission, but when atoms collide, it produces nuclear fusion, which releases much more energy. The planet Jupiter is also made of gas, but it's volume does not produce enough gravitational pressure for its gas atoms to fuse. Jupiter is a cold, dark place, while a star is hot, vibrant, volatile, exciting and is the center of it's own solar system! Now, ask yourself a question, is it by chance that people who serve on massive scales become *"stars?"* Such people serve on massive levels and truly become the best at what they do. The question is, *how do you get there?*

Now, I want you to take this concept of what creates a celestial star versus just a cold gas planet and apply it to yourself, another celestial body. As humans, if we want to become a *"star"* in our field, we must put the pressure on ourselves so massively, that we cause nuclear fusion *inside* of us that releases energy, skills and talents so much that our impact is guaranteed. We must set goals that are so massive, that the pressure is so great that we fuse inside. If the goals are just wishy-washy, pay-your-lousy-bills goals, your goals will not create the pressure you need to fuse and you will stay a gas planet, like Jupiter. But, if you want to be your own Sun, a star, then you must set and focus on a MASSIVE goal to create the pressure AND intentionally create the point-of-no-return. You must *"burn your boats."* According to Wikipedia, *"This alludes to certain famous incidents where a commander, having landed in a hostile country, ordered his men to destroy their ships, so that they would have to conquer the country or be killed."*[xi] This is the how you create the pressure required start fusing inside of you. This is the point that Santiago reaches in the book, *The Alchemist*, when he chooses to cross the desert on a caravan. Once he is a certain distance into the desert, he must look forward, because going back alone, without the caravan, would certainly kill him. The same is true of taking a sea voyage, you hit a point where you cannot swim back and must weather any storms that hit. Benjamin Disraeli said, "*Nothing can resist a will that will stake even its own existence on the fulfillment of a goal.*" To make your 'will' hit that point where your own existence is at risk if the goal isn't accomplished, is what you must do to create the pressure necessary to fuse inside.

By fuse inside, I mean hit a point where your vision is one of singularity. It is where you really get The Universal Law that your thinking is your future and take total control of what thoughts you have and which thoughts you apply emotion to. It is where you push aside ALL other distractions, hobbyist desires, white noise, undesirable relationships, and just focus on your main objective/your top task/your main goal. This is a position in which you must put yourself only if you want to succeed massively. You can easily create a hobby business that pumps out enough cash flow to pay your bills. You can do that in a short period of time. I am talking about actualizing your full genetic potential mentally, physically, spiritually, relationally and financially. Basically, to take your life as far as you can and to live as big as you can. In order to do this, you have to create your vision clearly, then only give mental real estate to YOUR VISION and only spend your time on tasks that are creating the vision you hold in mind.

This is exactly why Arnold Schwarzenegger is Arnold Schwarzenegger. He is a great example because he was the best in his field at multiple stages of his life. Arnold hates plan B! He says to make a full commitment, without a safety net. He says it is actually dangerous to have a plan B because you cut yourself off from fully committing. By fully committing, I think Arnold means that you don't put yourself in this position to feel the real, full pressure needed to create fusion within you. You need to hit that point, where you must give your current goal all you are capable of, because if you don't, you will literally starve. The only way to do that is to fully commit to it where you only look forward to what you can do to meet your goal, not backward at what you do *'just in case'*. Having any thoughts of *'just in case/plan B'* takes your thinking off of your vision and without your full mental energy focused on your vision, your fusion engine will continue to spark, but stall, because you do not have the required pressure to cause fusion. With a plan B, you remain a cold, gaseous planet like Jupiter and never create the sheer massive goal volume and point-of-no-return necessary to create the pressure required for your fusion engine to start up.

You may worry that if you don't have a plan B, that you may fail. Arnold mentions that there is nothing wrong with failing, that we should not be afraid of losing and both are necessary to climb the ladder. We discussed already that failure is not failure, but the exact stepping stones on your ladder about which Arnold is speaking. As you start to take action on your inspirations, don't be afraid of losing or "*failing*"! Really, do the best you possibly can, but don't be paralyzed by fear to not act. Take action and you will figure out what works and what doesn't.

In my business, I tell my customers that marketing is testing. We have certain core methods that we perform, but we have to get the combination of those that fit their industry that maximizes their return on investment. We have to try things to see what works, see what gets responses and do more of those things. In your life and business, you have to try things, then focus on what works. The things that don't work are a necessary part to finding what does. Robert Kiyosaki recommends that people, "*Fail*

Faster!" Meaning, to do this exact process to try things, stop doing what doesn't work so you can find what does work. The concept of understanding that the stepping stones are a part of your journey to find your channel of service is what leads you to the skill of abandoning your ego so you can dump the things that don't work and keep moving forward to find what does.

That is what I love about the vision show, Shark Tank. It shows people starting a business around their creative visualizations. Some ideas are awesome, some need work, but it doesn't matter. Taking the risk and trying is what matters. If a venture doesn't go as planned, so be it. You may have to work various jobs to pay back some debts from your venture, but consider the lessons you learn in any endeavor where you owe some money, the price of the lessons you learned. If you ended up debt financing your business, or learn another lesson in business that costs you money, consider it like paying for a semester of college. If you are taking action to try your creative visualizations, you are in the right direction and you will learn the skills that you need along the way.

On Shark Tank, Mark Cuban said, "*I would rather work 80 hours a week to make $50K and work for myself, then have a $75 to $100,000 job working for someone* *else."* Again, we all start by working for others for a period. The difference in owning your own business, however, is that you don't make the $50K forever, you make $100K the following year, then $300K, then much, much more. Also, you can delegate the work. If you gain customers for someone else's business, they own the customers, not you! This is the key to understand. When you own the business, as long as you continue to provide great service, you keep your customers and grow new customers. You can delegate tasks and develop systems to run your business, then put people in charge of those systems. You cannot scale if you don't own your business. When you do work for someone else, give it all you have, set goals for your work and adhere to and improve the company goals, but, and this is a big but, have your own goals and vision that you are working on outside of your job! Then, invest what you make at your job into your own business. What I want you to take from this is to always do your best at any place at which you find yourself. The key is doing your best each moment, be it at your job, then when you are working on your own goals.

I went all in on my businesses, meaning, there was no safety net, and there still isn't. The first few ventures I started did not go as planned and because of me going all in, I ended up in some debt. It took me years to pay it back by working six jobs at once. In my business and life, I know that I have to be an effective person to succeed each day on my goals. I know that if I break Universal Laws, that if I don't live my Unifying Principles, or if I slack off, that I will be back to working six jobs. So, guess what, I keep myself in check and get to work every day and effectively manage my business. To put it bluntly, I don't perform low priority tasks and am not lured into activities and people that take me away from working on my goals.

Eric Thomas has a story he tells where he had a friend who cut grass. When other friends would ask this guy to go out late, he would say, "*I have to cut Mrs. Jones' grass tomorrow.*" His friends would laugh at him and say, "*Cutting grass? Come on!*" He went home and went to sleep so he could get up early and get to his highest priority task, cutting Mrs. Jones' grass. Now, this guy makes close to a million dollars a year. I don't think his friends are laughing anymore. This guy had a clear goal and his goal was more important than what his friends thought of him leaving early. Once your vision is clear, this same process will become apparent for you and the decision to choose to work on your goals will be easy. When you have this attitude and just show up to work, over a period of time, you, too, will make millions.

Remember, success is the progressive realization of a goal. The Grand Canyon was formed by a little stream over time. Even if you work for 15 minutes per day on your top priority goal, you will experience the feeling of success and enthusiastic energy release of which I speak. This concept of becoming a star is meant to let you know how to create the pressure necessary to bring out of yourself talents and disciplines you would not have discovered if you did not *burn your boats*. Also, on the television show, *Shark Tank*, the investors always ask if the person is full-time before investing in the business. The reason why, is that they want to know if the person is fully committed. If the lead entrepreneur isn't confident enough to fully commit, why would someone have the confidence to put their money into that business? They don't. With full commitment many things happen that we can't explain. In the words of William Hutchison Murray:

"Until one is committed, there is hesitancy, the chance to draw back, always ineffectiveness. Concerning all acts of initiative (and creation), there is one elementary truth, the ignorance of which kills countless ideas and splendid plans: that the moment one definitely commits oneself, then Providence moves too. All sorts of things occur to help one

that would never otherwise have occurred. A whole stream of events issues from the decision, raising in one's favor all manner of unforeseen incidents and meetings and material assistance, which no man could have dreamt would have come his way. I have learned a deep respect for one of Goethe's couplets: Whatever you can do, or dream you can, begin it. Boldness has genius, power, and magic in it!"

The person you want to become is ultimately up to you, again, your choice. Choose what you want to put in your vision, then, use the tools in these pages to create your vision and become that person in the present moment. If you want to experience the fusion reaction we discussed, I encourage you to take Goethe's advice and to be bold in your goal setting, vision creation and daily vision achievement.

Remember, this 3% of the population that succeeds does so by the exact same process we are discussing here. They do it by creating a vision and holding that picture in their head. Then, whether they can articulate the process or not, they are following Universal Laws. After Bob Proctor read *Think and Grow Rich* by Napoleon Hill, he succeeded massively in business. He then wanted to know what changed and why he succeeded. He spent all his time after that question surfaced understanding the exact process we are going through here. Creating a clear vision, being grateful for that vision and taking action toward goals based on your inspiration, is the path. It is really that simple.

When you wake up every day, it is you who look at yourself in the mirror. Only you know if you are living your life in a way that makes you fuse inside, or a way where you feel like you have more to give. Trust me on this, all you have to do to start releasing energy is to get clear on your vision and work on your highest priority goals. Creating and holding this mental image and working on your new goals may require some new skills, but you will learn them. You really have three choices when it comes to this topic of creating fusion inside of you. Again, let's use the analogy of a celestial body of gas:

1. *Dissipation and death*: This happens when there is no pressure on the gas, the gas just dissipates and the celestial body dies. This is exactly what happens when one takes the goal setting and achievement pressure off of themselves in "retirement". Many times, before retirement, their vision and goals were given to them by their company and a boss and once they are no longer

in the employ of that organization, they also no longer have goals, aka, pressure. When the daily goal setting and achievement pressure is removed, their gas dissipates and, statistically, die after three years of retirement. From HuffPost.com, *"Study after study has shown that people who retire early tend to die sooner."*[xii]

2.   *Choose to be a gas planet*: From the Instagram user, thewaveandtheocean, *"Until you get very clear on what you want, you will get something that sorta-kind-almost-but not quite meets it. Keep refining with each experience. It is creating clarity."* This is what is meant by setting *pay-your-lousy-bills goals*, as Anthony Robbins says. This is what happens when you are not clear on what you want. This is what happens when you have 'general' goals like, happiness, a functional car, an eventual relationship, a place to live, workout when I can, etc. If you are not clear, you can't have exact tasks and without exact tasks, you get lost in the daily trivia of daily life. Without setting the goals of the life you actually desire, the goals that are so big that they get you out of bed excited; goals that create enough pressure to force you to fuse inside; you remain in a cold, dark state where you don't take that critical step to really do your best. That step where you,

for example, if you want to be a singer, start singing in public; going to open mic nights; renting halls; contacting agents; sending your demo tape out, etc. On the show, Shark Tank, Season 6, Episode 25, there is a gentleman, Mont Handley, president and CEO of PittMoss who comes on the show. When Robert Herjavec asked, *"How did you come up with it? I mean it is so creative."* Mont said, *"Robert, I have been interested in commercial greenhouses and don't ask me why, since I was a little kid. I bought my first greenhouse when I was 12 years old. My parents didn't even know I did it, and my mother was like, "I can't believe you sold a greenhouse to a 12 year old boy." My first job out of college was managing five locations of a retail nursery, and that's where I came up with the idea. I turned 50 this year, and I said to myself, "If you do not do this now, you will never do it." And that is why I said, "You have to do this."* At the very end, after Mark Cuban, Kevin O'Leary and Robert Herjavec invested in his venture, he said, *"This means that I can actually make a living, building on a dream that I have had for 20 years, and that is a really amazing feeling."*[xiii] And he started crying tears of joy. Mont Handley is the perfect example of a human being who chose to put himself in a situation where he was forced to fuse inside. He went from a gas planet, to a star by going all-in and creating the pressure necessary to fuse. A part of his fusion was him having the intestinal fortitude to put all of his money into his venture, then stepping onto the World Stage by applying and going on Shark Tank. He is a wonderful role model for how to create this fusion reaction inside. Also, at the end of the episode, when he cried the tears of joy, it just shows how The Universe works and how we are rewarded for having faith to pursue our talents, vision and ambitions. This release of tears shows the exact emotions and intensity created through full commitment to your vision. You can experience this same success, too.

3. *Choose to be a star*: The third choice we have is to put ourselves under enough goal pressure, as Mont Handley did above, to actually cause the fusion reaction inside of us about which we have been speaking. This is when you choose to go all in to living the vision you have created. Yes, you may bump around for awhile to figure out the intricacies of where the demand is, figuring out your exact channel of service and tweaking the business part. Yes, there may be a little adjustment period for a period of time, but

once you properly setup the business around your service, you focus on it in lieu of everything else. The more pressure on you, the better. The more pressure, the more fusion, the more energy released and the bigger you will get. If you have a lot of monthly bills, good! They will make you even hungrier, more focused and more effective in focusing your valuable time on only activities directly bringing you to your realized vision. A client of mine is a forensic accountant. He always recommends that a person in college take out loans because of the financial accountability it creates. I had student loans, and guess what, I put a passive income asset in place to pay that payment. Me having the financial accountability forced me to create the business services, systems and to make the sales through many intense conversations with clients explaining why the services we offer have value, why to go with us and why to stay with us. Without the financial accountabilities, I would never have developed such skills. The more accountabilities you have, the more pressure and the more you will fuse! As you create a bigger vision, you are going to have more financial accountabilities and you will be forced to fuse even more so you can generate the cash flow to pay for your increased vision.

It is your choice to what you want to become! You can take the pressure off, dissipate and die, which I consider to be hell on Earth. You can choose to live in a fog, with no goals or un-clear goals and just exist to pay bills, which is what most of civilization does. I would consider this purgatory, where you are not here nor there and just exist without fulfillment and a lifestyle that is not particularly motivating. Or, you can get laser focused, set big and bold goals, create massive pressure and fuse into a star, this is Heaven on Earth. You are not competing against anyone either! It is you who has look at yourself every day in the mirror. This is a great poem by Peter Dale Wimbrow, Sr. that my good friend shared with me in college:

The Man In The Glass

When you get what you want in your struggle for self

And the world makes you king for a day

Just go to the mirror and look at yourself

And see what that man has to say.

For it isn't your father, or mother, or wife

Whose judgment upon you must pass

The fellow whose verdict counts most in your life

Is the one staring back from the glass.

He's the fellow to please – never mind all the rest

For he's with you, clear to the end

And you've passed your most difficult, dangerous test

If the man in the glass is your friend.

You may fool the whole world down the pathway of years

And get pats on the back as you pass

But your final reward will be heartache and tears

If you've cheated the man in the glass.

At the end of the day, you have to live with the person you are. You can make the choice to live your vision at any time. You do not have to wait 20 years to live your vision either! Do it continually! Learn the skills in this book to set goals, make them your vision, listen for inspiration, act on your goals/inspirations, then achieve those goals and reset new ones! I highly encourage you to have a *final reward* you are proud of, one where you can spread your arms and say, "*Look at what I have created.*" It is up to you to take the time and make the effort to create and live your vision so you can enjoy the life that you designed, that you truly desire and one that will fill you with fulfillment each day you open your eyes.

It is Your Responsibility to Create Your Vision

Earl Nightingale once said, *"People don't think. If most people said what they were thinking, they'd be speechless."* By creating your vision, you are creating the substance of your thinking. I am very grateful to some of the excellent teachers I have had in my life and for them teaching me how to accomplish goals on a disciplined course. Schools are amazing at teaching students to accomplish goals, but there is a gap in the education industry of teaching the students to create their own goals and vision. Think of your own education, did you have any classes entitled *Personal Goals* or *Vision Creation*?

Schools were created to teach students basic content through an organized curriculum.[xiv] Employers look to school systems and universities to fill the work-force. The bells, schedules, and structure were created to replicate a work setting where things had to get done, like in a factory. Things like mandatory attendance; how to be efficient and how to get assignments done are examples of factory-type thinking. I am not saying this about education in any bad way. You could also describe the current educational model as systems thinking. Systems are what get things done so we can enjoy the quality of life we do, from running water, to electricity, to food in our refrigerator. Schools are excellent at teaching this. For example, Asa Packer founded Lehigh University to train engineers and managers to run his rail business. Schools were designed for students to learn a pre-made syllabus of basic information by having them perform tasks assigned to them and testing them on this information. Creative thinking is considered a byproduct of this process. Colleges are often ranked by their career placement after the student graduates. The value of a school is often placed on the ROI (return on investment) of the salary of the job a graduate would receive upon graduation. The skills taught in school are very valuable and can be a foundation to get your goals accomplished. Use all the skills you learned from school, sports, being a part of clubs and your social interaction to work on your goals daily. The goal of this book is for you to set your own syllabus and to use the systems thinking you were taught in school to execute your personal goal syllabus.

I know, from personal experience, and from giving goal setting and vision creation workshops at many universities, that students are never asked to set their own goals. When I said I was starting my own business right out of school, many people thought I was crazy. I had this mechanical engineering degree and an MBA, why wouldn't I use them to 'get a good job, with a good salary' many people asked. I saw my father, after working for a company for 30 years, be let go after the company was sold, and getting a six-month severance package. My father was grateful for the years he was there and the salary he received. I was just shocked at the abruptness of how fast things changed. This experience, and a few more that I had in my life, led me to uncover the Universal Law that I should own my own business, so I started one right out of school. This Universal Law is summarized by Brian Tracy quite well when he says, *"The more you seek security, the less of it you have. But the more you seek opportunity, the more likely it is that you will achieve the security that you desire."* The opportunity about which he is speaking are the creative visualizations you have.

The reason I bring this up is that you have to live your vision, no matter what the influences around you say. You will have some in your life who are supportive, and others who will blatantly laugh at you. It is imperative to believe your vision to be true and to not focus on those who don't support you. They are going to be there, but you must move forward no matter what. Fred Smith, the founder of FedEx, received a C on his paper about FedEx. He persevered and created FedEx. Don't listen to the naysayers, believe your vision to be true in the present moment and surround yourself with a peer group who supports you.

I had people who were supportive and people who thought starting a business was like a joke and that I should have used my education to work for a big bank or an engineering firm. Here I was, Tom Roman, going out and starting a business? Yes, I was unique at the time, but I was lucky to have had great role models and some really great teachers. I listened to Tony Robbins and did his goal setting courses. I read Robert Kiyosaki's books and learned to invest in cash flow producing assets and not spend money I made with my time on my luxuries. I was lucky, too, that after deciding to start my own business, that certain teachers I had really inspired me. One of my instructors placed the first order for my first business; another professor helped me with an independent study focused on my first business; and the Lehigh Athletic Department placed an ongoing order for athletic awards from us, for these gestures I will be forever grateful. Yes, there were some that were not supportive, but I only focused on those that were. After that, I spent years learning and creating businesses with residual, monthly income models and my business passive income produced more stable income than my bills in about a decade.

Being financially free does not mean that work is not required each day. If you are not growing, you are dying. There is no standing still. I recommend creating business models that lead to freedom for you, but any going-concern, be it an investment in real estate, the stock market or a business, requires management and work to keep going. The moment you stop setting goals to improve your business and your customer's lives, someone else who is hungrier will go out and take your customers and leave you in the dust. A part of having independence is to have the time to pioneer new ways of doing things, to improve your business' services, and to help your customers further reach their goals. The first goal to get to this independence is to simply have your business profit be more than your monthly bills. Once you do this, you achieve independence, but you must stay hungry, work hard and continue to innovate. If you don't, you will lose customers and be out of business in short order.

Our website hosting business, HostRoman.com, hosts a lot of websites and emails. A part of this staying hungry is when we made the commitment to 100% reliability in email and offering massive inboxes. We did a major migration that took over six months to complete. Since we finished the migration, we have not had any, not one, issue regarding email. We also upgraded our servers to the singular best servers that exist and upgrade them every 18 months. The reason why, we know that if we don't offer the best, our clients will go elsewhere. The hosting we offer includes the very best in SSLs (secure socket layers), website speed due to ram and solid-state hard drives, and simply the fastest uplinks in the industry. Staying hungry and continuing to offer the best services is a cornerstone to any company that wants to grow and I encourage you to always set new goals as your vision comes true, so you can dominate your industry and attract new clients in the future.

In the beginning of starting my business, there were stepping stones, many of them and years of lean financial times. People would often say, why don't you get a job and put this '*suffering*' to rest? Why? I knew another Universal Truth, that I had to always pay my phone bill, car payment and insurances. I knew that if I let another entity, such as a job, pay for these, that I would get used to it and I would become reliant on the income made from that job. This is what I consider '*taking the bait*', e.g. when a person gets a job and then makes financial commitments based on the income earned from their time in that job. In the movie, *Joe*

Versus the Volcano, when (Joe) Tom Hanks quits a job he says, *"And why, I ask myself, why have I put up with you? I can't imagine but I know. Fear. Yellow freakin' fear. I've been too chicken shit afraid to live my life so I sold it to you for three hundred freakin' dollars a week!"*[xv] I know, making the jump to living your vision is a big one and there may seem like there are a lot of factors to consider, but I encourage you to do it anyway. Use the experience you have and take the leap. Trust me, you can do it. Have faith and know that The Universe wants to create through you and your unique talents and when you take the risk to do so, with a grateful vision, you will be rewarded. Don't be afraid, have faith, and create the vivid, abundant, succulent and blissful future you want to experience through the exercises in this book.

If you find yourself in a situation where you have a lot of overhead and rely on your job to pay your bills, don't worry. If you want to live your vision, you will. Because of your financial commitments, you will stay even more focused on your vision and gratitude for it. You will have more of an incentive to work extremely efficiently to manifest the creative visualizations you receive through sound business practices. You will get to your vision even faster because of the pressure in which you put yourself.

Your vision will be even bigger than you imagined because with your intensity, you will extract from the ether what you need even faster! Trust me on this. I have seen people take the risk to live their vision and each time I have seen someone take that brave step, it always works out for the best and the person thanks God that they did it each day after. Their life is more exciting, bigger and just more interesting due to the fact that they chose to stake their claim. There are several examples of people who chose to live their vision later in life in this book. Follow their lead. If you are alive, there is time, and plenty of it. I encourage you to gratefully create your vision and listen for inspiration. Then, when the time is right for you, take action!

Somehow, by the Grace of God, through my readings, experiences and just by luck, I figured out to always put a cash flow producing asset when taking on a liability. To define them, according to Robert Kiyosaki, an asset puts money in your pocket, while a liability takes money out of your pocket. Ideally, it is better to put the asset in place before you take on the liability, but sometimes, opportunities and life happens where you take on the liability first. In that case, you have to really hustle to put the asset in place to pay for the luxury you are now

152

enjoying. One time, I saw a car I really wanted, so I financed it. Within a month, I closed enough hosting business to pay for the additional car payment and over several years, the car was paid off. Either putting the asset in place and rewarding yourself with a luxury, or getting the luxury and hustling to put the asset in place will work and different circumstances warrant different ways to purchase things. One way to purchase things is like a cafeteria, where you pay before you eat, as Brian Tracy says. The other way, is like a restaurant, where you eat first and pay after. Both work and it is up to us to choose on a case by case basis. Either way, I encourage you to create a business that produces monthly cash flow. Taking the path of having a business that could produce such cash flow was much, much slower in terms of having material items on the outside, but when I did get luxuries, such as cars, apartments, homes, etc., their monthly payments were paid for already through cash flow created from my business. Financial liabilities are a good thing and hold us accountable to getting up and focusing on our vision and business. The key is that you start and have cash flow producing business to pay for your luxuries.

I was very lucky, too. I was able to study and work at the *Iacocca Institute* for four years during undergrad and graduate school. I was lucky that I met many entrepreneurs through the *Global Village Program* and really contemplated my future. The career services department at Lehigh had a speaker, Patrick Combs, who wrote a book called, *Major in Success*, that really inspired me, too. He also introduced me to the book, The Alchemist, by Paulo Coelho, that inspired me to go for it and live my dream.

In school, students are fed their curriculum and may or may not be asked to create their vision. If a student is not asked about their specific personal goals, it is still their responsibility to do this on their own. The schools are brilliant at getting students to get the tasks in that curriculum completed and learned. However, they may lack the formal exercises to have their students creatively think about what they want to have in their life, the way they want to live, the things they want to have and the services they want to perform. I know this because I see it when holding a goal setting workshop to adults and students alike, where I ask, *"How many people here have clearly written goals and a plan to accomplish them?"* and literally, out of groups of 100 or more, one or two raise their hand! As Bob Proctor reminds us, another irony is that, as students, we are punished when we start having creative thoughts in class and that it was called daydreaming. I am encouraging you to listen to the creative thoughts you have and to act on them. Creative thought is *The Language of the Universe* and should be cultivated. As children we should be asked what we were creatively thinking, instead of punished for it and brought right back to regurgitating information. We should be encouraged to create those thoughts! I am encouraging you to do that here in this book. See the value in education! Get all the education you can, but focus your studies on skills to actualize your vision, aka your creative thoughts! Education should be a life-long endeavor, too. Constantly listen and read material leading to enhancements in skills and attitude, and also try to attend an immersive event, a weekend, at least once per year, to get you re-charged. There is something about the energy of immersion with other like-minded people to get jumpstarted on creating new goals and enhancing your vision.

When it comes to education, as Bob Proctor asked his kids, its not *"Are you going to college, but where are you going?"* If you have the opportunity to go to college, go! The more education in life the better and we should use the skills and disciplines learned in attaining higher education in the execution of our goals. Think about it in terms of time. Say you took two night courses a week that were four hours of time, after commuting. Now, schedule the same time to work on your goals, instead of taking the course. That would be 8 hours a week, or 32 hours a month. That is like an entire working week of just working on your goals! This is what is meant by scheduled time to work on your goals. Use the disciplines you developed in school to focus your energy on actualizing your vision! During the time actually spent in school, it is imperative to think for yourself and to set goals that lead to a clear vision. Then, every, single project you do, to apply it to YOUR VISION, not to some miscellaneous project assigned to you. This is what I did, what Fred Smith from FedEx did, and I encourage you do to the same. Remember, you are paying the professors and University for the privilege of being educated and you have the right and power to direct your studies toward the realization of your vision. This book is about creating and living this vision for yourself, your OWN vision, not permanently becoming a part of your teacher's, your school's or your job's.

You may have to maneuver your syllabus a bit to do this and get some professors to help sign off on your projects, but do it anyway. Many people say that you don't need college and that it is really expensive. This is a very hard topic because, although I agree, that all of the information can be found on-line, there is a coaching/mentorship/friendship aspect of college that does not exist in doing it all on your own. I know, for a fact, that I use many of the skills I was forced to learn in college on a day-to-day basis and am very grateful for all I learned from my professors and teachers over the years. I have an engineering degree and my Masters in Business Administration, both of which serve me immensely in running my business, and serve my clients through our services. I just know I never would have gone into so much depth and pushed myself so hard if I wasn't pushed by the syllabus and professor. I equate this concept to doing a workout in your home gym versus going to a CrossFit class. Yes, you can do it on your own, but you are guaranteed to get pushed to your limits when you are surrounded by others and also coached. Education is a continual process and getting all of it you can and always continuing to educate yourself is my advice. I have to put a disclaimer here as well. We ALL have to be a part of someone else's vision for a time, and when you are, do your absolute best in that situation. It is imperative, however, to have your own vision and goals towards which you are working and to put the effort from your studies and money from your 'job' into cash flow producing assets that pay for your luxuries. This is the path to financial independence and daily fulfillment.

You have to realize that teachers work very hard and do a great job at their profession and for this we should all be extremely grateful. I encourage teachers to also craft and live their vision. When it comes to your vision, however, please take a moment to remember that schools weren't really formed to help you think of your own goals and become financially free. They were designed to fill the workforce, not to help each individual create and live their vision. The people who own companies look to schools for qualified people to run their businesses. The 20th century school was literally designed by the same architects as prisons, run with the same schedules as factories, and adhere to a very rigid, standardized curriculum. Again, this format helps you learn how to get stuff done! School helps develop your work ethic and teaches you to have the discipline to complete your tasks. Use the task completion skills you learned in school to work daily on your goals, to manifest your vision and to run your OWN company! Remember, entrepreneurship is just a skill, like learning a language. With some practice, you will be great at it! Be grateful for having the opportunity to be educated, but don't expect or feel bad that the information on how to create your vision was somehow held back from you. The educational system was simply not designed to teach it. The above paragraph is a reality, but this book was not written to change education, it was written to help you create your goals and vision, then to gratefully hold your vision in mind and take action on the inspirations that ensue.

Your responsibility is to actualize your vision. Understanding that you can't change another person is a huge realization in life. Your only responsibility and the best you can do is to make the most of your life! My responsibility is to creating and cultivating my OWN vision. I was inspired to write this book as it was an inspiration to me when thinking and feeling gratitude for my vision. The vision seed I am creating, and choosing daily, is a that of an oak tree. My writing this book and sharing it with you is me cultivating the soil. By acting on my inspiration through writing, then choosing to share it with you as a form of service, I am doing my part on God's Plan. Me taking my inspiration and creating it is the BEST I CAN DO at this present moment.

Your only responsibility is to create and cultivate YOUR vision. It is up to YOU, personally, to create your goals, then to turn those goals into your vision, then to THINK about your vision as much as possible. It is up to

YOU to then get emotional about it and associate your vision with the strongest emotions possible, love and gratitude. Think of Mont Handley and how much love and gratitude he had when he expressed his tears of joy that he had the financing to live his vision and serve the world with it. Have this same passion and commitment to your vision! Keep your vision in mind, then, it is up to YOU to wake up and get to work on YOUR goals. That is it. If you do this process as the number one priority in your life, your life will drastically change and the exact vision you defined will materialize in your life in the very near future. I know, because I experienced this exact process in my own life. Everything on my vision board from a few years ago now exists in my life. I am constantly re-setting my goals and refining my vision as my goals are accomplished.

You may ask, *"What about leadership to my family and my community?"* Remember what Galileo Galilei said, *"We cannot teach people anything; we can only help them discover it within themselves."* When you are *"Living Your Vision"* through this process, your cup runneth over. Living your vision is the ultimate act in self-love because we live our life with a true feeling of fulfillment as we are doing what we were put on Earth to do. The energy released, as you take action on your goals, affects everyone you meet in an inspiring way. Giving material things to others thwarts emotional development and entitles, thus damaging their life. What, then, can we give others? What can we do to lead others? By living our vision, we give others the gift of our energy AND the inspiration of the example of our life. We show, through our own abundance, what is possible when we listen to our desires and wants, set goals, get clear on our vision and work on our goals daily. Truly, the best we can do is to live our vision, whatever that is, thus making the most of our lives. The real '*gift*' we can give others is the example of a life well-lived, then to inspire and validate them to do the same in their life.

Marketing genius, Dan Kennedy, says that a major key to success is to be a motivational personality. By living your vision, your release of energy and life example, make you a motivational personality by default. The best way to live your life is to be a source of motivation, not an ATM machine to those around you. People want to be inspired, encouraged and validated to create and live THEIR vision, not have their skills stolen from them by being given that which they should do themselves! Being a motivational personality gives the inspiration for others to live their vision themselves, while giving materially robs them of the tools of independence.

I want to emphasize again that it is a well-known universal truth that we become exactly what we think about. Just as our bodies literally become what we eat, our speech is a window to our thinking and our life is the reflection of our thinking. Our life becomes exactly what we think and our thoughts are completely in our own control. It is our personal responsibility to create the substance of our thinking through goal setting and vision creation. Then, to reside in a state of gratitude for our vision through mental exercise and visualization.

What is Mental Exercise & Visualization?

It is widely believed that humans only access 5% of their minds. You have access to *100% of your mind*. 5% is the conscious mind and 95% is Universal Mind, the subconscious mind or God's Mind. Our brains are a jelly-like grey matter the size of a grapefruit, but it acts as a radio by creating the frequency with which we communicate with The Universe. We impress upon this infinite mind with our conscious thoughts. Our thoughts are the seeds that attract from the ether the inspiration, events, conditions and people that form the very vision we hold in our thinking. It is time to plant the seed of the life that you want and hold it in place with love and gratitude. Setting your goals and thinking your vision will require effort, like going to the gym. Please examine the feeling you have after you work on your goals. It is like the feeling you have after you take a shower post workout, but even better! You will have an energy released through you that is, what I believe, THE peak emotion that life offers.

There is a story that Earl Nightingale tells about a farmer who is standing at the edge of his property when a driver stops and speaks to him. The driver says, *"That's a nice farm God has blessed you with.*" The farmer stops what he is doing, leans on his shovel, and looks at his beautifully manicured farm. He responds, "*Well, thank you but you should have seen it when God had it all to himself.*" The farmer worked hard to cultivate his farm and the same is true with our mind. The real joy is unleashed when we cultivate our minds and exercise it to its full potential. The job of the conscious 5% is to keep the vision in the forefront of our mind of what we want clear and steadfast. The 95% that is God's Mind or Universal Mind will then germinate *our* mind with inspirations and put the exact circumstances in our path that will help realize our vision. If we simply hold our vision in mind, inspiration will surface. From there, we define our goals and develop a scheduled action plan for accomplishing those goals one by one. Once this action time is on our calendar, we simply need to show up. In addition, as amazing as this sounds, all manner of people, events and circumstances will organize themselves to allow your vision to materialize, seemingly out of thin air.

There will be moments that you notice proof that there is a bigger plan of which you are a part and how perfect it really is. You will notice something that you bought years ago, then, a project you are doing requires that exact thing.

You remember buying it and then, all of a sudden, you need it. It seems like a miracle, but this is what happens, over and over again! Everything just falls into place at the right time, exactly as needed for your vision to unfold! Another example of this that brought tears to my eyes was when I was in the basement of our new home. I printed out my vision board and was hanging it up in our home gym. On the vision board was a photo of the interior of a home with a wood ceiling, mind you, I have only seen a few wood ceilings in my life in restaurants, but never in a private home. The new home we just purchased had a wood ceiling, even more beautiful than the one on the vision board. I literally dropped to my knees, with tears of gratitude in my eyes, looked up into the sky and just said, *"Thank you, thank you, thank you!"* You will experience the same types of synchronicities in your life as you gratefully think your vision and act on your inspirations. Your only responsibilities are to hold your clear vision with gratitude, to set goals, then take action to realize your inspirations and goals. That is it, you just have to do those few things.

A story that I think really illustrates gratitude is one that I use in my goal setting workshops. Think of this scenario... Say that you gave me a five-dollar Starbucks gift card as a present. When you gave it to me, I looked at you and said, "*I don't really like Starbucks, it is too strong, I prefer Dunkin Donuts.*" How would you feel? Honestly. Perhaps you would be like, "*What an ingrate! I am never giving him anything again.*" Then, it would take some time to recover from such a toxic event as giving someone a present and them being ungrateful for it. One thing is for sure I think, you would never get me another gift card. Okay, let's erase that situation and start over... You give me the Starbucks gift card and I smile hugely and give you a massive bear hug. I say, "*I LOVE Starbucks, thank you so much for thinking of me.*" Then, a few days later, you get a nice thank you card in the mail. You may think, "*It was just a $5 gift card, this thank you card is beautiful and probably cost more than the $5!*" You go and post the beautifully written card on your coffee table and go on with your day. Then, a few weeks later, we run into each other. I say to you, "*I really want to thank you for that gift card. Really. The day after you gave me that gift card, I went to Starbucks and got a large cappuccino. Normally, I would just opt for a coffee, but since I had that awesome gift card, I went for the good stuff. On the way to work that day, I hit a major traffic jam, one where I had to put the car in park. I opened the sun roof of my car, and as the sun warmed my* *face, I sipped my cappuccino. Immediately, I was transported to a Parisian sidewalk café and my heart and soul warmed my entire body. When I got to work that day, I immediately booked a trip to Paris. Thank you for inspiring me and for your generous gift, it made a big difference to me and my life."* Then, I gave you a big hug. Now, let me ask you a question. In the first instance, when I said I didn't like Starbucks, how did you feel? Did you feel like you wanted to give more, or did my ingratitude push you away? Now, for the second example, how did I make you feel? You would probably want to get me a $25 gift card, or even buy me a several hundred-dollar cappuccino machine, right?!

Our relationship to other humans is the same as our relationship to The Universe. When we give the gift of gratitude to another, they WANT to give us more. When we appreciate our spouse for all they do, they WANT to make special dinners, buy flowers and do anything they can to make your life better. When we are grateful to our friends, they WANT to talk to us and share experiences. When we are grateful to God/The Universe for all we have and for our vision, The Universe WANTS to give us more! The Universe will give us the inspiration that will bring the material means to enjoy the vision we desire. At the same time, our accomplishment of these inspirations, will fulfill us more than anything possibly can. Ingratitude is like trying to hold the two North ends of two magnets together, they repel and will never attract each other. When you are grateful, it is like the North and South ends of two magnets touching... They SNAP together with such voracity, it is almost startling. When you express gratitude, you literally relate to everyone in an attractive manner, including The Universe. When you relate to The Universe in this way, you unlock the flood gates of creative thought and inspiration as The Universe wants to give you the cappuccino maker. You have to ask yourself if the attitude you have inside is one of gratitude or not. If it is, you will get the cappuccino maker, if it is not, you literally intentionally drive yourself away from ever receiving future gifts. It is up to you to show up to life with a grateful spirit and attitude. This choice is completely in your own control, no matter what your life conditions are. Viktor Frankl proved this when he chose his attitude of mind, even when in a concentration camp during World War II. Read his book, *Man's Search for Meaning* to learn how and why he chose his attitude, even in the worst conditions any human being has ever experienced. If he chose his attitude, so can you!

Actor Woody Allen once said, *"80% of success is showing up."* How true is this concept for anyone who has ever committed to an exercise program at a gym? We may not feel like going to the gym each day but when we do, we simply do the workout. The key is just showing up. If we show up, ten times out of ten, we *will* exercise and results will come in accordance to the effort we put in. The same concept applies to thinking gratitude for our vision and working on our goals. When we have clear goals and a clear vision, then simply put time in our calendar to work on them, then show up and just take action, our entire life changes. We become an *Energy Releaser* after we work on our goals. All we have to do is simply show up, in gratitude, to experience these remarkable changes in our emotional life and life conditions.

In his book *Essentialism,* Greg McKeown talks about a survey where people on their deathbed were asked what they would have changed about their lives. The overwhelming response was that they wished they had lived for themselves instead of always striving to meet the expectations of others. Years ago, I had an amazing conversation with a man whose company made cemetery tombstones. He told me to do what I wanted to do with my life because eventually we all end up in the ground. I told him, *"Okay."* He stopped, put his hand on my shoulder, looked at me in the eyes and said, *"No, really, do what YOU want with YOUR life."* What great advice! *How right is he?* I want you to really get this point that creating your vision and living it is within your grasp and will release a life that is hard to imagine at this moment, but trust me, it is there waiting for you. I know this sounds morbid, but think of yourself in a casket one day. Picture being lowered into the ground, with wet, cold soil shoveled on top of you... THAT is the only time when living your vision is too late. Even when you are at that state, you should, as Mark Victor Hansen recommends, *"My dream for the end of my long life will be that I have not yet achieved all of my goals. I hope the same is true of you."*[xvi] Literally, when I went through some of the valleys of my life, what really pushed me through them was when I thought of my potential and all of the people I could serve. When I thought of my potential, I was like, *"All I have to do is get through this little patch and I will have the privilege to use my talents to serve many people."* When you have a numbered list of goals, you can't wait to get up in the morning and work on them. When you are on your deathbed, you will be like, damn, I have more to do, not atrophied and wondering what show is on next! Walt Disney had such clear goals that a goal of his, Epcot Center, was built seventeen years after his death![xvii] If you are alive, take action now! TODAY, do the exercises in this book, create your vision board, re-write your goals, and become the person in your vision today, in gratitude! Truly, I tell you, there is NOTHING to lose and a life of amazement to gain. Create and focus on YOUR vision! When we focus on our vision, then spend our best energies on accomplishing OUR high priority goals, our lives become on fire.

What do I mean by *'best energies?'* I mean to work on YOUR personal goals at times of the day when you have the most energy. For me, it is first thing in the morning, even before breakfast, with a fresh cup of coffee. At that time, before the business day starts, before everyone is out of bed, that I am truly on fire! When we simply focus on our high priority goals, we become like the Edisions, Einsteins and other names on the *muster roll of civilization.* The moment we get clear on our wants and desires through our goals and vision, then do what we were put here to do, we become just like them. The only difference the people you read about and you is that they worked on their goals each day. They didn't become Edison in one day, it was thousands of days of him working on his goals, solving problems, and persevering that led him to uncover the

Universal Laws he did. You have that same exact power!

We can connect to a channel or frequency higher than ourselves and allow whatever that power is, to flow through us and create. All you have to do is work on your goals, and in the intricacies of working on your goals, magic will happen, and things will click. You will be given access to the *Gifts of the Universe*. You will see combinations of things that you never saw before, you will discover new Universal Laws as Einstein and Edison did. Once you get a feel for creating your vision by working on your goals, you will have a burning desire to get started each day. This process opens up a direct channel to Universal Mind. Do this regularly and you will feel wealthy and release energy you never knew existed. Work on your goals daily and your mind will become a channel for Universal Mind. Your hands, feet and mouth will become the very tools the Universe uses to further Its evolution.

In the world within, us *thinking our vision* is the magnet that attracts to us powerful inspiration. These inspirations show how to achieve that which we desire. The Universe/God is so benevolent that He/She wants to give us exactly what we want. Think of prayer. When we speak a prayer or think it silently, the mind creates a visual representation about that which we pray. In that moment, with our conscious mind, through our mind's images, we are telling God exactly what we want. However, the 95% of our mind that is God is listening *all the time* and not only when we bow our heads or between the blessings. This is why all thoughts - no matter when we think them - count towards realizing our vision. If we present our desires to The Universal Mind clearly, we will be provided with the inspiration and opportunities to manifest the thoughts we hold in mind, no matter how big they are. **Mark: 11:23:** *For truly I say to you, whoever says to this mountain be taken up and be put in to the sea; and has no doubt in his heart but shall believe those things which he said shall come to pass; he shall have whatever he said.*

Remember the analogy of the seed. If we plant a seed for poison ivy, we will grow poison ivy. If we plant an acorn, we will grow an oak tree. Choose, right now, to be the seed of an oak tree! The type of seed you are is determined by the thoughts that you think. Want to grow into a multimillionaire? THINK thoughts with gratitude as if you are a multimillionaire. On the contrary, want to always struggle and be broke financially and emotionally? Okay, simply parrot the thinking of the media and others in your life without clear goals and visions.

There is no higher range of human emotions then when

you think of your vision and work on your goals. Our emotions are not only controlled merely by our thinking, but by our acting as well, so you want to do both. Think powerfully and act powerfully. Do you feel better after hitting the gym? Of course you do. Our thinking leads our action, and our actions also lead our emotions. When you have gratitude for your vision, then take action on goals that will lead to your vision, you will release the best feelings that exist to human beings. Thinking is only one part of the equation. The equation goes like this: Our thoughts determine our actions and actions create our conditions. Therefore, let's get clear on our thinking, which determine our actions, which creates our life conditions.

The following sections of this book will help you to create clear goals and to define your vision. The exercises you will go through will:

- Instantly improve your self-esteem by thinking about your accomplishments
- Help you realize that everything in and around your life was once a goal and, therefore, you've accomplished many things in your life already through this process, but now we are going to formalize and accelerate it

- Develop an attitude of gratitude about all that you have to bring yourself in harmonious relation with the Universal Mind/The Mind of God
- Create a foundation on which to build your life by creating and living, what Benjamin Franklin termed, Your Unifying Principles
- Set goals and keep a clear vision about that which you want to experience in life
- Create a physical vision board of pictures and images to display in your home that represent your goals and dreams
- Practice gratitude for your what you have AND your vision as a deliberate way of life
- Schedule time into your daily calendar to work on your prioritized goals

The exercises in Part IV will provide you with the tool of ***thought substitution*** and strengthen your relationship with Universal Mind/God. Thought substitution is based on the theory that the mind can only hold one thought at a time. The key is to have our vision so clearly defined that we instantly identify those thoughts that are undesirable and think of our vision instead. As Mr. Schwarzenegger explained, we must have a clear vision *first* and then *grow* into it. All we have to do is think, believe, and feel that our vision has manifested. Too often, we allow regretful thoughts or vision-hijacking people to interrupt our day, thwarting our vision and stopping us from working on our goals. The next time this happens, practice substituting these negative thoughts with thoughts of gratitude for what you have and your vision. Thank God for His perfect plan for you. Take a moment to appreciate that you are exactly where you are supposed to be on your journey. Then, simply gratefully refocus on your vision and get back to work on your goals.

In the next section, I will also share with you a process for stretching and massaging your mind so that your personal psychology is one of power. Wallace Waddles once wrote, *"More important than what we read is what we think about what we read"*. The exercises in Part IV will help you reach deep into your mind, soul, and spirit to create the life you desire. Remember, emotions are determined by thoughts and actions so by harnessing your thinking and actions, you harness – and, thus, control - your emotions/vibration. By getting on the emotional vibration of your vision, you will bring inspirations to accomplish it into reality.

As you move through these exercises, be patient with

yourself. If you've never been consistent as a runner, attempting to run a 5K would be extremely difficult. However, if you start out slow, building up gradually over a few months, running the 5K would be no problem. The same theory applies to your mental muscle. Unless you've been consciously and consistently focusing on a vision for the future, your mind naturally is busy with random thoughts and daily trivia. Robert A. Heinlein once said, *"In the absence of clearly-defined goals, we become strangely loyal to performing daily trivia until ultimately we become enslaved by it."* This is true of the news, social media, politics, personal relationships, our job or any of the trivialities that can take us away from our vision. Anything shiny and new easily distracts, so the practice of having a clear vision and thought substitution takes some practice. Retain the power to choose to reject thoughts that are not in line with your vision and substitute them with your vision. Then, simply get back to work on your goals and I guarantee that your conditions will change. Mental exercise is an "inner game" activity that most people neglect due to life's endless distractions. This neglect leads to erratic thinking, a very, very foggy vision and lack of focused action. In this abundance of choices at our fingertips, most people are incapable of choosing wisely what to do with their time if they don't have a clear vision.

In academia, we accomplish our goals to meet the requirements of various educational curriculums. At the start of the school year, we receive our textbooks along with a syllabus that tells us exactly how to complete the work. Initially, the assignments given seem overwhelming but somehow, at the year's end, we manage to get it all done. Chapter by chapter, test by test, in a very organized manner, we meet our educational goals, learn an entire textbook and master our finals. Teachers do an excellent job at holding us accountable for learning the required material and, for this, we should be grateful. We can meet our personal and professional goals in the exact same manner by simply using what we already know. For those who struggled in school, this is the time to refresh your memories of how it works - prioritized tasks, one at a time. This time, however, the process will also include getting in touch with your true wants and desires. When you do, the overall benefits will go beyond what you have ever imagined.

It has been said that the real work needed to develop and succeed in business typically occurs before 9am and after 5pm. This, of course, is because the hours in between are devoted to serving customers. I know, it sounds like a lot of work, but I ask that you think of it another way. When you set your own goals, you can't wait to work on them! When you are truly engaged in creating your vision, you literally want to finish your client work so you can work on your highest priority task. When your vision is clear and you are working on your goals, you will be itching to get back to working on your next task!

In school, it was the teacher's job to show us how to follow a syllabus and complete the assignments to meet the daily goals. Now, it is up to *you* to create your own syllabus and assignments to create the life that you want to live. To live our vision, we must master the creation and execution of goal setting and this does not happen by focusing on the many trivialities and distractions that have been placed all around us. Greg McKeown illustrates in his book, *Essentialism*, that *we can either go a millimeter in a million directions or go big in one direction.* I am pushing you to go big by teaching you how to make goal setting and goal getting, top priorities in your life. The scheduling of time is the starting place for this. Accomplish your goals one at a time and move down the list. This action helps you to build habits that lead to success. As you begin to live your vision in the flesh, as you put pressure on yourself by setting big goals, reach them, re-set them, add the new goals to your vision and continue to create and serve on greater levels, you will have an energy released from you that will feel like nuclear fusion! You setting goals puts pressure on you to cause this nuclear fusion. Again, without pressure, the Sun would just dissipate into the space around it. Without intentional focused pressure, our minds dissipate and atrophy.

It is up to the individual to be clear on what he or she wants out of life. Our desires are unique and represent God's attempts to breathe through us. These desires are our birthright and we have the ability to experience each one to the fullest. In the following sections we will go through a course for an amazing life by putting the theories of visualization and goal setting into action.

Part III: Visualization

Consider this section as a personal trainer for developing a ninja-like ability to think your vision of the life you want to live and how to take action on the goals you set.

There are some simple steps to this process:

- **Goal setting:** *taking the time and effort to think about and define what you truly want*
- **Vision creation:** *transforming your goals into pictures, then a mental image… your vision. Finding photos in magazines, online, etc. and hanging them in a place that you see every day. I personally recommend placing them on the front of your refrigerator*
- **Practice:** *Practicing visualization via frequency, duration, vividness, intensity and gratitude*
- **Mental ownership:** *Taking mental ownership of your vision by practicing gratitude as if your vision is already true*
- **Prioritize and finish goals in order:** *Accomplish your vision by prioritizing your goals in order of importance, then working on them until completion before starting on the next one*

- **Schedule goal time:** *Putting time in your calendar for taking action on your goals with certainty and gratitude that your vision is on its way*

It is your job to transform this thinking session into a personal system for priming your predominant mental attitude. This new attitude will enable you to take absolute mental ownership of the present, the future, and the journey therein. To be successful, your new thinking system will require daily attention. In the morning and at night, please practice with discipline, dedication, passion and faith to emphasize your vision and fully impress it onto Universal Mind/The Mind of God.

How often do you exercise to maintain good health? How often do you shower to maintain cleanliness? How often do you brush your teeth to maintain good oral hygiene? How often do you eat to maintain energy and metabolism? How often do you think appropriate thoughts to maintain your vision? For most people, the answer to each question will vary from once per day up to six times per day. Your job is to exercise your mind with the same frequency as you perform any of the aforementioned activities. Consider these mental exercises as a way of clearing your mind of unnecessary clutter so that you can re-fill it to the brim with only thoughts that you want to manifest in your life.

To achieve our vision, we must guard our minds like a hawk, only allowing in those thoughts that are beneficial to our psyche. Use street smarts and discernment for all situations, people and stimuli and remain committed to the truth that your vision is real. Understand that most news stories are nothing more than staged, fictional nonsense intended to sadden and shock the viewing public. The purpose of TV, in general, is to spread propaganda and to cater to advertisers who want to do your thinking for you. In fact, the intention of advertising has never been to convey truth. Advertising was specifically created to manipulate behavior to get you to buy their products. All media between commercials is simply there to get you to watch the commercials. Mental exercise to focus on your vision, with practice, will strengthen your mind and create a barrier against the world's unnecessary clutter.

Make it a goal each day to keep your mind naturally full of thoughts based on the concepts of abundance and prosperity. This thinking process builds a natural protective barrier between you and the malevolent intrusions of the mainstream media. Personally, I went on a media fast over a decade ago and have not looked back. Now, I laugh at the boundarylessness of the daily news headlines and I am never taken in. As Steve Chandler says, *"...knowing that the only goal of modern media is to shock and sadden us"* allows me to stay in perspective.

Our thinking is the seed in the soil of our soul that attracts inspiration. Another way to put this is that thinking enacts silent demand. We ask for things directly through our thoughts. Clear, orderly thoughts yield clear, orderly results... this is *silent demand.* Your mind is given inspiration and life conditions correlate to the thoughts you hold in your mind. The seed does not ask the soil for nutrients because there is no need. Instead, the seed simply connects to the soil harmoniously to acquire whatever it needs. In this same manner, we can plant a seed of thought and simply stay focused, using the methods below, and see our vision grow before our eyes. Taking mental ownership is believing you already have that which you visualize in gratitude. It is through gratitude that you harmoniously relate to The Universe and naturally and effortlessly receive exactly the thoughts you need from the ether around you, just like the seed. Gratitude is the key to the entire equation. Do all you can, anything you can, to practice gratitude. The inspiration we attract ultimately comes from keeping our vision gratefully and clearly in our mind. Through our spoken word and physical actions, we plant seeds within our current condition that physically manifest into what we desire. Clear and orderly action yields the life that we want. With our thoughts, we can overcome all obstacles. As the words of Voltaire wisely remind us, *"No problem can withstand the assault of sustained thinking."* Also, give the ideas that you do not use to someone who can benefit from your inspiration. The act of giving away ideas is a wonderful form of service!

When your thoughts are in a state of gratitude towards your vision, you are living as if your vision is here! You are taking mental ownership of your vision as if it were already true. When you are in the state in thought that your vision is true and are in gratitude for it, your words themselves are inspirational. When someone asks how you are, you literally feel, awesome, great, fantastic, terrific! Once you start living the life of your vision by taking the appropriate actions, you will feel utterly successful and incredible every day, all day. As Arnold describes, this journey begins inside in our mind. Taking action on our goals forces us to grow into that life.

Mental Exercise

This mental exercise involves *believing* that we are capable of doing what any other human being has done in history but *multiplied*. Visualize great leaders, artists, musicians, authors, your parents, your teachers, mentors, business and community leaders, presidents, and inventors. With intensity, take a moment to focus your thoughts on these people. Imagine how they behave in all facets of their lives including at work, with family, and at play. Think of this bible verse from **John 15:13:** *Greater love hath no man than this, that a man lay down his life for his friends.* Give thanks to these people for having the courage to lay down their lives, time, and talents on the path before you so that you, too, may follow your vision. Be confident in the fact that you have the same abilities.

Imagine William Shakespeare writing on parchment with a quill, *"To thine own self be true, and it must follow as the night the day, thou canst not then be false to any man."* Today is your time to be true to yourself and to take vigorous action toward your goals.

In your mind, picture Benjamin Franklin thinking, writing, and speaking as an inventor, businessman, friend and diplomat. Ask yourself why Benjamin Franklin was so influential. Ben Franklin believed that life was short and there was no time to procrastinate. He chose to serve the people through business, community, government, and through the writing of an autobiography filled with his life experiences. You have that same ability.

Mother Theresa dedicated her life to serving the poor. You can serve others in your own way. Gandhi was a moral prodigy. You can be a moral prodigy.

Wallace Waddles once wrote, *"Remember Lincoln in the dark days of the Civil War. He alone furnished a supply of faith and hope for the nation."* You, too, have the power to furnish hope to all those around you by your life-example of living your vision.

Visualize those whom you have admired throughout life and give thanks for their courage and ability to lead. Allow these people to become the peer group of your mind's eye. Alongside your vision board, collect photos, paintings, busts and other visuals of these chosen leaders to display prominently in your home or place of business. In life, we become the average of our chosen peer group. Create a future tile, to be discussed in depth later, for your peer group, too. Davinci, Michelangelo, Edison, Mother Teresa, Einstein, if you want them as your peers, put them in! Let these visual reminders encourage you each day to strive for the same capabilities and beyond.

Meditative Visualization for Health & Vitality:

The following meditative exercise and the short sections that follow are paraphrased from the book The Science of Being Great by Wallace Waddles:

Sit comfortably, relaxing your mind and body with thoughts of health and vitality. Concentrate on breathing deeply and quietly from your abdomen while repeating the healing affirmations (in italics) below:

Spinal Cord & Nerves: *My nerves are in perfect order all over my body. Each nerve obeys my will and brings me mental tranquility.*

Lungs: *With every breath, I purify my blood and move air into every cell of my body and lungs*

Heart: *My heart beats strong and steady, improving circulation to all of my extremities.*

Digestive system: *My digestive system functions perfectly. My food digests and assimilates to rebuild and nourish my body. I am what I eat. My kidneys, stomach, liver, and bladder perform perfectly, keeping me healthy and well. My* *body is resting and my soul is at peace.*

Mental Health: *I have faith in my health, my finances and in all other matters. I am perfectly well in every way. From within me, God uses my hands, eyes, nose, ears, taste, emotion, and touch to create all thoughts and experiences. Through God, these things impel toward me. God speaks through me and grants all that I desire. I have faith and courage and know that the best that has ever been, is right now. I know God appreciates the best he and others have created through me and my senses that is why I desire to experience the best in my life.*

I rise above all temptation, loving everyone and everything unconditionally. I realize that being grateful makes me full of greatness and I hold love, peace, serenity, and understanding toward all living souls.

I only perform right actions and follow those courses in accordance with my highest ideals. Each day, I will do right, think right, and speak right. I will be the creator and appreciator of all things great.

Attaining the Ultimate Attitude:

Your attitude reflects your view of the world and universe. To attain the Ultimate Attitude, your view of the universe is harmonious and all-encompassing. In your mind, the world and all it contains is expanding and improving. You believe that you are exactly where you are supposed to be, making excellent decisions, and that your past is your syllabus. Each day is about doing the continuing the evolution of The Universal Plan. From this place of love, your life, wealth, health, and relationships will exponentially expand and improve.

Creating the Ideal Viewpoint:

The universe and world are perfect. The world, as you see it, is always advancing forward in perfection. Only from this ideal viewpoint will you contemplate the facts of social, political and industrial life. Behold, it is all very good. You now view all human beings – family, friends, acquaintances, and neighbors - in the same way. Nothing is wrong with the universe and nothing *can go* wrong except for my own personal attitude. Henceforth, I will strive to keep the right attitude and ideal viewpoint at all times. I have complete faith and trust in God and His Plan.

Learning to Surrender:

For all challenges, turn to God. Understand that a Power walks with you and through you on this journey.

When times are challenging or when you grieve, have faith that He carries you. Search within to see the right in all things and project this to your outward life. What you outgrow, abandon. Surrender the body to the mind, yield the mind to the soul and give the soul to the guidance of God.

Finding Spiritual Identification:

There is but one substance and source and you are one with it. You are made of the same substance as the Universe. Surrender yourself to conscious unity with the pure power that flows through you through gratitude.

Crystallizing the Vision:

This is the entire point of this book. FORM YOUR VISION. This mental picture of yourself is you at the greatest height of your imagination. Dwell upon this picture with regular frequency at the longest duration of which you are capable. Then imagine your vision with frequency, duration, vividness, intensity, and gratitude, holding the thought that *this is who you really are.* This image is a reflection of your soul and from this perfect image, you now manifest outward and your life conditions will soon be exactly the vision you now hold in mind. Once you create your vision, you must do everything in your power to become that person NOW, in the present moment. When you become that person, feel like that person and live as that person, your emotions and vibration ARE that person. The time to manifest your vision it is only a matter of being consistent in this vibration and taking effective action and finishing the projects that you start with the inspirations you receive.

Realizing Your Power:

You, alone, possess the POWER to become and do anything you want. You realize that your desires are gifts to you from an Eternal Power. Exercise your creative energy on your goals to achieve full power and energy release. Arise each day and go forth with perfect confidence. You will do mighty work.

Expressing Gratitude:

Feel grateful for life and your vision. Look at the gifts God bestows upon you with great appreciation. Think of the best and better will be given. In this mental state, you are connected at the highest vibration. You will create and perform amazing service. Choose to be grateful for your present experiences and gifts bestowed upon you and hold gratitude for your vision.

Choosing Forgiveness:

Choose to forgive all people and even those who do not seek forgiveness. Most importantly, forgive yourself. Love everyone and everything unconditionally, realizing that holding onto low vibration emotions only hurts you. Hold thoughts of peace, love, and understanding toward all living souls and always act in accordance with your highest ideals. With the understanding that from thinking come conditions, you choose only to think and feel the best thoughts and emotions possible. Remember, however, that forgiveness does not mean you have to continue to be in contact with those you forgive. If someone abuses you, forgive them, then go no-contact so you can stay focused on your vision at the highest vibration possible and also help them continue to develop on their emotional journey. Think of Saint John Paul the II and how he forgave the man who shot him, but he did not continue having contact with him.

Living in Faith:

Real faith involves surrender and humility. Believe that you are exactly where you are supposed to be and that you made all past decisions exactly as you were supposed to according to your level of awareness at that time. Understand that the lessons you've learned on your journey make up your education. There are lessons to be learned from every life experience. The struggles, grief, and adversities that occur are simply preparation for further skill and character development. Whenever doubt surfaces, simply remind yourself that you are exactly where you are supposed to be and focus on your clear mental vision.

Creating Strong Boundaries:

Boundaries serve as our personal protection. Although the world is perfect, there are people who continually exist in a spectrum of states of emotional, mental, and physical development. When dealing with people, understand that any loss of power that you feel is due to the breaking of a boundary or an attempt at abuse. Although this behavior is not always intentional, you must draw a boundary as if you are dealing with a child and commit to its enforcement. Symbolically, realize that in the art of skillful negotiation, certain cases may dictate that you walk away from the negotiation table if the other party is incapable of handling the conditions of your boundary. Feel empowered by walking away because you showed self-love by not tolerating bad behavior toward you in your life. By going no contact, you also did the only thing possible to help them actually develop.

More importantly, however, you are making the choice to gratefully keep your thoughts on your vision, thus emotionally keeping you in the vibration of the life you want to experience. Remember the example of oxygen masks in a plane. You put yours on first so you can live, then you help others put theirs on. Your main responsibility is to make the most of your life, then, your example helps others do the same with their lives. You can't have your *World Within* constantly uprooted because of your relations with a toxic person or organization. If you want to experience the vision on the outside, you MUST keep your vibration stable on the inside. If someone chooses to be toxic, put your oxygen mask on and go no-contact with them. Then, continue to gratefully focus on your vision and take effective action on the inspirations you receive. Creating boundaries and going no-contact with toxic and poisonous people is a major part of self-love.

I know that this topic is mentioned several times in this book, but I really want to emphasize it. It took my entire life to learn that it is okay to not continue to relate to people who make me feel bad, attempt to be abusive and superior, or put me and those I love in harm's way. Yes, forgive them, but you do not have to have them in your life anymore. There is no veil to this rule either. Anyone who relates through methods that take you from your high vibration should go. This is the definition of crabs in the bucket, people who see you succeeding and do anything they can to pull you down. Them trying to pull you down is all you have to see and realize they do not have your best interest in mind. You have to have your own self-interest in mind and learn to love yourself enough to only allow people and experiences that bring joy into your life. You should implement a zero-abuse policy, or stated in the affirmative, a Joy Policy. Your Joy Policy says that you only allow healthy emotional people, experiences and organizations into your life that promote improved mental and emotional health. You are better off having a few close, emotionally healthy friends, then a large quantity of acquaintances where you allow toxic behaviors to get to you because of some sort of group dynamic. Do not let the snake through the grass and cut off toxic people before they say or do something that could permanently prevent your vision from being realized. When you get into this habit, you are giving yourself a gift of extreme self-love.

Choosing only joyful, healthy, validating and encouraging relationships will unleash a flow of power inside of you that you may have never experienced before. You will wonder why you didn't do it sooner.

Visualizing Greatness

In the section to follow, we will study how the *act of thinking* dictates goals, affirmations, visualization, and character traits. Our vision is our *present condition* in mind & spirit for which we must take mental ownership and have gratitude. The time is now. This will be a production thinking session where you will organize your thoughts. In doing this, you will gain control over emotions and take better action when serving the world. Productive thinking raises our emotional vibration and helps us to develop great speech and action accordingly.

You will also learn that planning your day is a fundamental key to success. You never see baseball players doing push-ups during a game but they certainly do *many* push-ups in practice. Great players *plan* to do great in the coming game. Practice the fundamental skill of planning your day *every* day and do it with joy and gratitude. Your thoughts, speech, and actions are who you are. Your daily plan is your roadmap to success. You must plan time each day to work on your highest priority goal.

Focus:

Esther Hicks wrote, *"Whatever you are thinking about*

is literally like planning a future event. When you're worrying, you're planning. When you're appreciating, you're planning. What are you planning?" In other words, what we think will manifest so we have to choose the content of our thoughts carefully and be fully conscious of our mental vision.

Now, visualize your favorite works of art. In your mind's eye, see the colors, the paint strokes, and the texture of the canvas. Now, paint in your own way today by putting your unique skills to work. Move your thinking to the physical realm. Focus on harmony. You are a great, enlightened master. As a business person, you train your organization to serve more people on a larger scale through business systems. As a philosopher and leader, you help others to believe that all things are possible. You have it within you to create a masterpiece and you can begin today! You recognize the enormous power and talent that exists within you. If your skills need development, know that God's power is there and you can call upon Him to help. The goal of this section is to show you how to call upon this Universal Power.

Russ Whitney said, *"Obstacles are those frightful things you see when you take your eyes off of your goals."*

What are goals? Simply put, your goals are a list of what you want to accomplish, ordered, in the numbered in their order of importance, ready to be worked on in your next goal time slot. To see your future, examine your goals. What Russ Whitney means is that we only feel fear when we are not working on our most important goal. When we work on our most important goal, fear dissolves and dissipates and what is left is pure focus, concentration, enthusiasm, excitement and power.

Paul almost singlehandedly spread Christianity across the Roman Empire. Paul's secret was a focused life. He said, "*I am focusing all of my energies on one thing: forgetting the past and looking forward to what lies ahead.*" It is time to create a future that is full of color and vitality on which you can focus.

As George Matthew Adams said, "*Learn to keep the door shut. Keep out of your world and universe every element that seeks admittance with no definite helpful end in view.*" Our personal universe is all that surrounds us. Fill your mind with thoughts of abundance. Allow only those thoughts into your world that will benefit your life of service. Focus only on thoughts that have the highest potential because, when combined with your actions, these thoughts will manifest, yielding high potential outcomes.

Visualization Is a Massage for Your Mind & Soul

Designing your future feels amazing! See your future by thinking about your goals. Goals are simply dreams that have a due date. Goals create the future *in advance*. Goal setting and achievement are fundamental to success and must be practiced daily. Embrace the fundamentals of goal setting and do your best to serve others through your unique talents. Understand that creating an awesome life for yourself is leadership in itself, your life is leadership. This means that your living your vision is enough to inspire those in your universe. Desires are inspired by and given to us by a power within. It is our job to transform our desires into goals and to create and be in gratitude for our vision of that life.

There is a saying, there is no vacation from your dreams. It is very much okay to be lazy about things, activities and actions not on the way to your vision. This day, you will only accept greatness in your mind and life. You will achieve all that you desire as you continually set goals, have gratitude for your vision and take daily action on the goals you have set. Life conditions are changed through action. Demand more each day from yourself than others expect.

To bring our goals to life, our emotional vibration and overall thought and emotional frequency need to synch up. This means that you must have mental ownership of your vision…to FEEL as if your vision is already true and to become that person. This section will explain how to become the person who has already accomplished his or her goals in the present moment. Goals are not about what you get but about *who you become.* Become that person in your vision NOW! Focus on what really matters, your vision. You *can accomplish anything* by practicing the thinking and action formula described here. Your thoughts dictate who you are, what you want, and who you will become in this life. If you want greatness, think greatness and speak greatness.

Remember, the greatest among us shall serve. While acquiring nice material possessions is certainly desirable, you will realize that the real accomplishments are those you can contribute. Your real goals will be achieved through serving others and your greatness will be defined by how *well* you serve. As Thomas Carlyle said, *"It is not what I have but what I do that is my kingdom."* The material stuff that you have – aside from the basics of food, clothes, and shelter, is fun, and necessary. You need a car to get places, and you might as well have a car that makes you smile when you start her up, but, as my Dad says, one comes down the assembly line every sixty seconds. What ultimately gets us up in the morning is the desire *to do, to create, and to make* something that can only come into existence through us. As Bob Proctor reminds us, the body is the instrument of the mind. The beauty is that we don't need special tools or certain conditions to serve others. You can serve greatly by simply doing your current task on your prioritized action list and doing the best that you can *today*. As Anthony Robbins says, *"Clarity is power"*. In other words, welcome to your spot amongst the *"3% of people"* who have a clear mental vision. All we have to do is visualize (or think, dream, and imagine) the life we desire and then schedule the time to make it happen.

If you desire a future that is colorful and absolutely compelling, it is time to create some goal-setting pressure. The more pressure, the more energy you will release and the bigger the diamonds you will create! Want an example of someone fusing at a massive scale? Look at Anthony Robbins. He is a powerhouse and is the epitome of someone who put huge amounts of pressure on himself and who serves on humongous levels. The pressure he put on himself causes the fusion reaction and is what makes him perform at the top of his field and serve millions. Time to create some focused pressure in your life! Perform the mental exercises in this book each day and then take action as if you are the person who achieved your vision today. Act as if success is the only possible outcome!

Setting the Goal to Become a Millionaire

Paraphrasing Jim Rohn: "Set a goal to become a millionaire, for what it will make of you to achieve it. The million is automatic. It is the person you will become to earn it. Not only in economics. You will become:

- A problem solver

- Knowledgeable

- A person who understands the market

- Someone who can overcome difficulty

- An early riser

- An expert time manager

- One who learns to develop their part on The Universal Plan

- A person utilizing their talents where your services have demand and traction in the market

Wealth is a state of mind. People *feel* wealthy or they feel the opposite. Our goal here is for you to feel wealthy and vibrate wealth while your skills develop and grow. Your character is forged, not given. Your life consists of trial, tribulations, and learning experiences. Every successful person has had to endure a barrage of peaks and valleys. Most millionaires made and lost their fortune multiple times before acquiring the necessary skills to make the money stick. If you are alive, then there is time to do it. Colonel Sanders was 65 years old and reliant on a $105/month Social Security check when he incorporated Kentucky Fried Chicken. [xviii]

As Robert Collier says in *The Secret of the Ages*, "*No one need retire to the chimney corner, no matter how many years have passed over his head. Years should bring wisdom and greater health - not decrepitude. Many of the world's famous people did their greatest work long after the age when most men are in their graves. Tennyson composed the immortal lines of "Crossing the Bar" at the age of 80. Plato still had pen in hand at 81. Cato learned Greek at the same age. Humboldt completed his "Cosmos" in his ninetieth year, while John Wesley at 82 said 'It is twelve years now since I have felt any such sensation as fatigue.'* The state of your age is equal to the clarity of your vision. You are as young as looking forward to working on your next goal. It doesn't matter how wealthy you get either! Having a clear vision and working on it as soon as you get up in the morning is what keeps you young and full of energy that you release to others! Remember that having goals that create pressure in our lives will cause fusion inside of us. Just like the Sun. Without pressure, the Sun would go out and it's gases would just dissipate in space. You need to keep the pressure on to continue to fuse and create energy, motivation and fulfillment!

The moment he learned that he was the highest paid actor, Dwayne Johnson said, "*The wolf is always scratchin' at the door.*" I think he means that even though he is succeeding, that he wants to work even harder in the future, keep the pressure on and become even better. This is the exact attitude you have to have. Despite your vision manifesting, which has to happen as you work on goals, you have to continue to reset and go after new, bigger goals that, as Mark Victor Hansen says, "Hit homeruns for humanity." As you choose to be a goal setter and goal getter, your mind will get better with age.

Also, just because you can 'retire' why would you?? Pardon my French, but it sucks! Statistically, people die after three years of 'retirement' because their mind atrophies because they take the pressure off and no longer challenge themselves. I had enough cash flow to 'retire' at 35, but I wanted to be the best at what I did and help our clients be the best at what they do. Also, just because my bills were paid by the cash flow from my business, I knew that in order to follow The Universal Law that says to create energy through fusion, like the Sun, that I needed to keep the pressure on. I needed to set bigger goals and wanted to truly serve more people. I know that if one person has done it, I can do it, too. Whatever that power is inside of us, continues to push me forward and I inherently need to do more, be more and have more. I encourage you to do the same. I really want to emphasize that retiring is not the move and anyone telling you to do so does not have your best interest in mind! If anyone tells you to retire, what, they want you to die after three years? They want you to 'back out of life', as Bob Proctor says about retirement? Okay, you can afford it, so what!? You take the pressure off, you die! Think of anyone on the current muster roll of civilization... They work harder, long after the financial time they could retire. They serve more and BETTER. For example, aren't we all better and don't we all benefit for Dewayne Johnson continuing to act, despite the fact that he could easily afford to stop? If he stopped and retired, wouldn't we all be worse off? Imagine your favorite actor/actress, athlete, teacher, professor, etc. retiring because he/she could afford it?? Imagine if Ben Franklin retired, which he could have easily done, being the first millionaire in America. There is a high probability that America would not have happened if he took himself out of the game. He was 70 years old in 1776 and did all he could to serve others until the day he went home. Now, imagine you, truly engaged in your vision, with millions of people that you serve, or a handful of people you serve, retiring? The number of people doesn't matter, what matters is that whoever you serve, they would all suffer because of you choosing to step out of their lives! Imagine Tony Robbins 'retiring' and all the people who would lose out! When Dewayne Johnson, Tony Robbins or any person creating value on a massive scale works, they are serving others! This is what having a clear vision will do for you, give you the inspiration for service that when you perform it, you will feel amazing and could never even imagine 'retiring' because you love what you do so much, it is what you would choose to do even if you didn't have to!

Also, look at Will Smith, Dewayne Johnson, Sylvester Stallone, Judi Dench, Arnold Schwarzenegger, Meryl Streep, Bruce Willis, etc., they are all in the best shape of their lives and pushing harder professionally now than ever. Look at what Arnold did, he served as Governor of California for 8 years! Look at Sylvester Stallone, he is writing and starring in awesome movies and is in the best shape of his life! Talk about pouring it on! These are the role models we should have, NOT people telling you that you should be retiring at some point. Really, if the work you are doing makes you want to do NOTHING versus going to that job, CREATE YOUR VISION NOW and go live it! This retirement thing is such crap. I was lucky that I was able to work with Lee Iacocca during my 4 years at the Iacocca Institute. He clearly told me, on many occasions, to never retire! He, God rest his wonderful soul, kept creating awesome businesses until the day God took him home. Listen to the greats about continuing to serve others through new ideas, intellectual property and business ventures. Create your vision and put your eggs in the basket of your own venture, then, as Andrew Carnegie said, WATCH THAT BASKET!!!

Socking away money in a bank account is the opposite of 'The Parable of the Talents' from The Bible. The moral of this story is that we must put our money into service. When you start your business, you will invest in things that make your business function and bring your services to your clients, e.g. property, plant, people and equipment. Money in a bank account is basically doing nothing and only helps realize the bank owners' vision on the profit they make. Please realize that when you are working toward someone else's vision, you don't own the business, so the only asset you have is the money you make and that money in a bank account isn't doing much, that's why you don't make anything significant on it.

When you start your own business, potentially doing the same work you are doing now, and say you took on your former boss as a client, you would be doing the same work, but through your OWN business structure. When you do this, you can scale the business, take on more clients, write business systems, delegate, write books about your services, potentially give speeches and anything else you can imagine. You would also be building the asset of your own business, which could be worth a fortune. As you make money, yes, you save some, but you also invest in your business, creating a more valuable asset than that money alone could ever be. Yes, you are doing the same work, but according to your own vision and building your own asset. See the difference? I think putting our money into service has a much higher return than merely putting it in the bank. The use of money in business can bring tremendous value and service to others and change their lives. I truly believe this is what our ancestors and the Founding Fathers worked for, to give us the choice and freedom to choose to hang our own shingle for the best outcome for everyone involved. As a business, you can offer more specialized services as you can build a team where each person is the best at what they do. You can give the gift of this business structure to your team as well and inspire them to live their vision through your interaction. This is what every great leader does. Look at how many people say they worked for Jim Rohn, Earl Nightingale, Buckminster Fuller, W. Clement Stone, Lee Iacocca, etc. All the people who mentioned working for these people, Bob Proctor, Tony Robbins, Jack Canfield, Joe Vitale, etc., ALL own their own businesses and are outrageously successful. Please see how these great leaders all encouraged their team to go out and be the biggest and best they can be. You don't have to work for any of them to benefit from their wisdom either, just read their books and follow The Universal Laws they teach. You can create a business that is a mecca of wisdom, inspiration and a springboard to people living their vision, like these people did. You can have a team that all provide amazing services for your clients, who are able to do so with the structure we discuss here. One's desire to want to stop working and retire is really their desire to do that which the they want with their time. Forgive the double negative, but it is NOT NOTHING.

What that impulse to retire really is not retirement at all. What really fulfills is to spend time choosing to do what you want to do and it is NEVER too late to create that life. Choosing the service to offer is the very thing we hope to help you find in this book. The service that if you didn't need the money you would be doing with your time. I hope we can turbo boost the creation and manifestation of your vision so you can completely let go of the concept of retirement and have the burning desire to wake up and do what you want to do. Will it be hard? I don't know, were finals hard? Were they worth it? The comfort zone shattering experience you will go through will be an adventure. Think of Indiana Jones, did his adventures require some effort? Yes, but he was entering the unknown and that is what makes life exciting and why it is called an adventure. Each moment of living your vision will be filled with adventure, excitement and fulfillment as the work you are doing can only be done by you and you will experience the rewards emotionally and materially. You, however, are not the only people who will experience the rewards of you living your vision, so will all of your customers and The World. Think of when, for example, Dewayne Johnson, makes a new movie, you can't wait to see it and it is really awesome, right? You are caught in suspense, laughter and it is just a wonderful experience. The world will benefit the same way from your service as you choose to live your vision. My hope for you is that you spend the time to perform these exercises, to craft your vision and then, enjoy each second of your adventurous life. Again, look at opportunities in your current industry, where you can create a business doing what you are doing now. Present your own business structure to your boss and see what they say. If they say yes, great, if they say no, have no worries, you will find customers in no time. Whatever the service you choose to offer, keep the feeling of wealth in mind.

I encourage you to have a millionaire mindset. When you do, you are a millionaire in the creative realm and everyone with whom you interact will gain from the experience. In the physical world, one can become a millionaire at any time as long as the stepping-stones and challenges of the journey are handled correctly.

The mental exercises within this book apply to your soul, mind, and body. You can do it! You can reach each one of your goals. Benjamin Franklin once said, *"Energy and persistence conquer all things."* If you are consistent with your goals, you *will* grow into your vision because it *has* to happen. It is a Universal Law. Take mental ownership of your millions now as if you have it in the bank. Speak as a millionaire would speak. In this mental state, if someone asked how you were doing, there would only be one answer: "GREAT!"

Mirror the Millionaire Mindset with Your "Inner Coach"

If you want to be financially independent, you need to have the cash flow to live the life you desire. If you are thinking big, then think and feel the following affirmations: I am a millionaire. I think like a millionaire. I speak like a millionaire. I walk like a millionaire. I believe, feel and act like a millionaire. I eat like a millionaire. I serve like a millionaire. I drive like a millionaire. I jump out of bed like a millionaire, excited for the day, my goals and activities, and my plan for the service ahead of me. I am a millionaire problem solver. I am very knowledgeable and I know how to persevere, learn, and overcome. I enjoy clean, millionaire living by eating and drinking only the foods and beverages that promote good health spiritually, mentally and physically. I am a millionaire with how I manage my time. I speak like a millionaire by always promoting great vocabulary and promoting equality among all members of humanity. I follow Universal Laws as a millionaire as this one skill allows me to leave the harbor and explore the adventure. I am enjoying each present moment as a millionaire with total appreciation.

Practice Gratitude

Gratitude is the second highest emotion with love being the first. Our vibration is our emotional state, our emotional state precedes our actions, and our actions create our conditions moment by moment. Throughout this book, we learned that our thoughts dictate and lead our emotions. In order to maintain the highest mental vibration at all times, do all you can to focus on the things for which you are grateful. Gratitude is the state in which all good things come into your life. Consciously live in gratitude so that more good things can flow into your life.

We always have the choice to be in gratitude. All we have to do is to *remember to remember*. As Wallace Wattles once said, "*Gratitude is looking at the best in life and by looking at the best, we receive more of the best.*" We can see everything - every condition and institution - from the attitude of gratitude. For example, as Wallace Wattles reminds us, think of politics and be grateful. Without government, we would have anarchy and what we have is infinitely better than anarchy. It is in the mindset of gratitude that all good things come to you." It is our choice to see life from that state. Again, think of Victor Frankl in *Man's Search for Meaning*. As a prisoner in a concentration camp, he would give away his food to other prisoners. He learned that the one thing over which our control is absolute in our human psyche is our attitude of mind. He proved this and you will learn how to practice flexing your gratitude muscle in the exercise below.

How many times throughout the course of our daily life do we notice random pennies in our path? We see them everywhere - at home, in the street, on our desks, etc. In his discussions and writings about abundance, Wayne Dwyer, God rest his soul, asks us to think about the significance of this penny.

When you see a random penny, do you a) step over it and keep walking, b) say "Damn! Only a penny?", or c) pick it up and thank God for continuing to shower you with abundance. Which would do *you* do? By not picking up that penny, you are sending a message to the Universe that either you don't care about money or that you have enough and don't want more of it. Remember, the Universe does not judge, or differentiate. All the Universe sees is your vision and if you are grateful, if you are, you will receive more.

God showers us each day with abundance. We live in the golden age of civilization and it is only getting better.

We have more opportunities and choices now than any one who ever existed in the history of the world. When in a state of gratitude, you, as Wallace Wattles says, draw nigh, or near to God and more is given to you. When you are not in gratitude, you push God and more blessings away.

On a side note, the same is true in relationships. Think about what a relationship is, you want to be attractive, right? If that is the case, wouldn't it be smart to follow the Law of Attraction, which consists of being grateful and appreciative. When you are grateful and appreciative, your partner wants to give you more, as Dr. John Gray says in the movie, The Secret[xix]. When you are inappreciative and ungrateful, it is just inharmonious behavior that pushes your partner away and makes the relationship just not fun to be in. The same exact principle holds true with The Universe. When you are grateful and appreciative, The Universe gives you more, when you are ungrateful, that ingratitude pushes The Universe and more blessings in the future away. It is in our self-interest and a huge part of self-love and realizing your vision, to practice gratitude.

Gratitude Mental Exercise:

The purpose of this exercise is to show you how to move consciously to a state of gratitude from any other mental state at any time. Gratitude is an *attitude that takes some very minor effort to develop.* You have the choice of gratitude available to you at all times, in each moment. *Gratitude is wealth in action while ingratitude is poverty in action.* Below is a real time exercise to help you get into a state of gratitude.

To begin, take a deep breath. In your mind's eye, visualize all the people, places and things for which you are grateful. Do this slowly and with purpose. Take your time to move down your mental list. Your list may include your gratitude for family, friends, health, and God. You may feel grateful for your faith, your country, and for your ability to speak and interact with those that you love. You may be grateful for having a functional mode of transportation, the ability to throw a party, access to a running path, membership to a gym, and the ability to pay your bills. Breathe deeply while thanking God for your amazing body, mind, and soul. Give thanks for the food that you eat and the air that you breathe. God has placed you on a perfect path and he would never steer you wrong.

Be grateful for the ability to live life on your terms and for the opportunities in business that allow you to live a great life. Have gratitude for knowing and discovering your true purpose and doing your best everyday. Think of all the simple things in your life such as running water, electricity, food, heat, and air conditioning and take nothing for granted. *Think of it all and feel tremendous gratitude.*

As you feel gratitude, your quality of life and relationships will improve drastically. Where there was once discord, there is now harmony. As you practice gratitude, you will align yourself with Universal Mind and bring all good to your life for gratitude is gravity for good, it pulls all the best to you. Know that God or The Universe will give you exactly what you desire. This mind is objective and whatever your thoughts and feelings are, will show up in your future.

It is important to act in ways congruent with the best you can think. You do not need anyone's permission to think and act in ways congruent with Universal Laws. Actually, any person or organization who tells you to limit your knowledge on applying Universal Laws does not have your best interest in mind. That being said, sometimes, people still want to see that thinking a bold vision and believing in its manifestation is supported in their religious literature. I was raised Christian and my holy book is The Bible. The following quotes from the Bible emphasize that the new and old testaments encourage you to move mountains with your thoughts and goals. They teach that if we ask (through our thinking) then the door will be answered (in our life conditions). When we focus on gratitude in our daily prayers, meditation and thinking, we will be magnets for all the good we can imagine, and more than we can imagine. All we have to do is ask and we shall receive.

Here are some awesome quotes from The Bible that show how the philosophy of having a vision is taught in Christianity. You will also find such supporting quotes in whatever religion you research as these laws are Universal Principles.

Matthew: 5:5: Blessed are the meek for they shall inherit the earth.

Psalm: 37:11: But the meek shall inherit the land and shall delight themselves in the abundance of peace.

The meek are in connection to God. Meekness occurs when one listens to their soul and humbles himself or herself to do God's Will. Meekness is NOT being poor. Meekness is listening to the inspiration inside of you, then being humble enough to perform the work necessary to bring that inspiration to reality.

Mark 9:23: And Jesus said unto him, "All things are possible to him that believes it."

Matthew 21:22: And all things, whatsoever, yea shall ask in prayer, believing, ye shall receive.

The mental attitude of thought ownership is the belief about which Jesus is speaking.

John 15:13: Greater love hath no man than this, that a man lay down his life for his friend.

Those who listen to their inspiration lay down their lives in service to others by doing God's Will, aka, the inspirations they were given.

Matthew 18:20: For where two or more are gathered together in my name, there I am in the midst of them.

As we speak of God, he is with us.

Matthew 7:7: Ask and it shall be given you; seek and ye shall find; knock and it shall be opened unto you. For everyone that asketh, receivith; and to him that knocketh, it shall be opened.

Asking is your thinking/prayer. Seeking is your words.

Knocking is your action. Think, speak and act in congruence with your mental vision. The door opening are your life conditions changing.

2 Corinthians 6:16: For you are the temple of the living God. As God has said, "I dwell in them and walk among them"

God is inside of you. The inspiration you receive is God breathing through you.

Heb 11:1: Now faith is the substance of things hoped for, the evidence of things unseen.

Faith is evidence. What you think, you can achieve. Faith equals trust. Have faith and trust what you are going through is for your best outcome in all life conditions, no matter what you are going through.

Mark: 11:23: For truly I say to you, whoever says to this mountain be taken up and be put in to the sea; and has no doubt in his heart, but shall believe those things which he said shall come to pass; he shall have whatever he said.

THINK BIG!!! Set big goals and hold them in your mind as true by taking mental ownership. With this faith, you, too, will move mountains.

Matthew 23:11: He who is greatest among you shall serve.

Service is equivalent to greatness. God wants us to serve Him through serving others.

"Living a Life Triumphant" has been defined as living a life where we serve to the greatest of our ability - enough to fill an ocean - and take but a small drop in return to live our lifestyle.

I personally believe that we are instruments of a higher power. That we are God/The Universe's hands, feet, voice, eyes, ears, etc. Joe Vitale wrote in The Abundance Manifesto that PT Barnum regularly said, *"Not my will, but thy will be done."* Until I read this, I associated that phrase to when you are going through a tough time or are grieving to help comfort you, but Joe Vitale says it applies to the affirmative as well. Sometimes, God calls you to great things, sometimes you would rather not do, but have to, because you were called to do them. This is a great prayer that helps clarify this point: *O God, beloved of my soul, I adore you. Enlighten me, guide me, strengthen me, and console me. Tell me what I should do... give me your orders. I promise to submit myself to all that you permit to happen to me. Let me only know your will.*

I write of this concept of being an instrument to a higher power because I truly believe it leads to the highest realm of emotions. When we choose to submit ourselves to the work that flows through us, I believe that this is the best we can feel as human beings.

Channels of Service:

As the Bible tells us, if we strive to be great and fulfilled, service to others is how we get there. Albert Schweitzer said, *"One thing I know: the only ones among you who will be really happy are those who will have sought and found how to serve."* Our *channel of service* is the structure through which we bring our services to those who need them. We must continually strive to determine and refine our channels of service. Andrew Carnegie found his channel of service through what he called *grim necessity*. In other words, while forced to work lower level jobs to keep food on the table, he acquired the necessary business skills to start the greatest steel company in history. In turn, Carnegie became one of the wealthiest people on the planet. Albert Einstein, because there were no academic positions available, worked at a patent office after he finished his doctorate. He needed to feed his family and was grateful for the work. At the patent office, he studied the applications for the electro-mechanical time keeping systems of the Swiss train system. This job experience and intense immersion in time systems helped him theorize relativity. The inspirational stories of Carnegie and Einstein illustrate how almost any unexpected career path can lead to amazing success if people simply look beneath the surface.

To have humility and meekness means that we have accepted God's plan for us. It means that we are bending our knees to the Will of God. When one is meek and performs the service they are called to perform at the moment, he or she is in a state of connection where The Higher Power can flow through them. At this connected state, we are at our highest vibration. No matter what work you perform or how humble it seems, do your best with all the love in your heart. Successful people *learn to love* the work they do. Successful people do each thing they put their mind to with the best possible attitude they can. The successful restauranteur was equally successful as when they were a bus boy as when they owned 12 restaurants. Learning to be the best they can be at the bus boy position is what allowed them to ascend through to owning the restaurants.

Often, the most successful entrepreneurial ventures are born through ideas found in existing industries. Find a need and proceed to fill it by creating your own unique niche in the industry. The key to success as an entrepreneur is found in creating businesses with two key characteristics. First, that your business sells products or services that are billed monthly. This is so when you close a sale, you receive income monthly for the life of that account and you don't have to be constantly hunting to pay your bills. Second, that the services you perform are backed up by great vendors who manage the services or that the work can be delegated to your team. This ensures that you do not create a job for yourself, because, no matter how much you love what you are doing at first, work is work and you should setup a business model that has recurring monthly revenue and that can be delegated, so you can best serve your customers, scale your business and gain your independence.

Our ability to read the mind of God is evident when we experience creative thought or inspiration. It is through this reading of God's Mind that we *"inherit the land and ultimately delight ourselves in the abundance of peace"*. As you serve, ideas will surface in many different ways. Some people experience and refer to blinding flashes of inspiration as "seeing the light". Mark Victor Hansen refers to this phenomenon of creative thought as, *"new intuitions, inspirations, ideas, thought-forms, and hunches gushing into your mind."*[xx] When this happens to you, write down or record your experience. Inspiration appears to us in thought. Again, think of taking a shower, you are in a closed box, but ideas come to you through your mind. As Nolan Bushill, the founder of Atari says, *"Get out of the shower and do something about them!"* Humility is to serve in the way in which we are inspired, despite our training or education. When God gives us inspiration and we act upon that inspiration, we are allowing His Word to become flesh.

When we actualize our creative visualizations through action, we have created a channel recognized as *genius*. Einstein said *"thank you"* many times per day, connecting to God through gratitude. Do you see why his gratitude created the relationship for Omniscience to reveal to Einstein one of the most important Universal Laws of the 20th Century? If gratitude worked for him, it will work for you. To materialize our vision as rapidly as possible, the best we can do is to become an instrument of God through which omniscience can serve and appreciate. Our goal each day is to utilize our immense spiritual and mental power to reside in a state of connection. To keep this connection, you simply have to keep your vision in mind and hold gratitude for it in the present moment. As you face new situations, new abilities and solutions will be revealed.

Genius has nothing to do with education but rather it has to do with how well we learn *to think*. Work on your mental house cleaning and then add great thinking to the clutter free space. Clear out the white noise and only think about people, places, and things for which you are grateful. When you have made this connection, you can begin to visualize the life you really want. If you think greatly by having a vision, speak greatly, by having gratitude for that vision in the present moment and do greatly, by acting on inspired thought, you will *feel* great. This connection and process is what is meant by *"On Earth as it is in Heaven."*

Breaking Through the Mental Barrier

One of my favorite authors is Rhonda Byrne. She produced the amazing movie, *The Secret*, and also wrote *The Power*, *The Magic* and *Hero*. My wife and I listen to *The Power* on repeat when we are driving and doing stuff around the house. Everything about it is a just good, positive and forward thinking.

In the movie, *The Secret*, there is a scene when Joe Vitale states that some people have a belief that there is not enough in the world. Joe Vitale then goes on to say how there is enough because we all want different things. He mentions that everyone doesn't want the same car, the same vacation, or to live in the same place, for example. I often use this as an exercise in my goal setting and vision creation workshops to help people break through the mental barrier of thinking that they somehow can't have the future they actually want.

I do an exercise where I ask people to write down their top three desirable cars, vacations and meals. I ask them to be specific, down to the color, interior, etc. Not one time, out of thousands of people, have I ever received two identical answers. There was a time when two people said peanut butter and jelly sandwiches, but one was on white bread and the other on whole wheat! Not once, did two people want the same exact thing. Your desires are unique to you and the things you want, want you even more than you want them!

In the book, *Clutter Clearing with Fung Shui,* Karen Kingston writes how if you run out of something, you can just go to the store up the street to get more. There is something called '*Depression Era Thinking*' where people have a feeling of lack as if things will dry up and they clutter up their lives because of it.

I encourage you to break through any feeling of lack by knowing that what any person has done, you can do, too. This is why it is so important to read autobiographies and to surround yourself with busts of such notable people and to make them your peer group. If you became the average of W. Clement Stone, Andrew Carnegie, Thomas Edison, Mary Kay, Ben Franklin and George Washington, you, too would be massively successful. You can do what they did, multiplied!

Believe in Your Genius

Ralph Waldo Emerson said, "... *the heart which abandons itself to the Supreme Mind finds itself related to all works, and will travel a royal road to particular knowledge and powers. In ascending to this primary and aboriginal sentiment, we have come from our remote station on the circumference (of the earth) instantaneously to the center of the world, where, as in the closet of God, we see causes, and anticipate the universe, which is but a slow effect.*"

There is a misguided teaching that tells us we are not the center of the universe and that comparing ourselves to the geniuses of history is vain. I disagree on both counts. You should think of yourself as a genius! All we have to do is understand the difference between healthy self-esteem and narcissism. Your self-esteem represents how you feel about yourself as a person while narcissism is a personality disorder based on superiority and false entitlement. There is a huge difference between the two. The universe may be huge but we are made of the same substance as the stars. As you keep your vision in mind and are grateful for it, you will receive inspiration, as you act on that inspiration, genius will unfold before your eyes. Believe that you are important in God's plan and be humble enough to adjust your sails to the winds of change as new inspiration surfaces.

Also, take the pressure off of yourself. There's a humorous but true adage stating that the first sign of a nervous breakdown is to think that your work will change the world. Just do your best to think your vision every day in gratitude and do the work you are called to do. Just put one foot in front of the other, do your work today, and be humble enough to persevere by adjusting your sails as necessary. Bend with the wind and just do your best each day.

Creating Your Unifying Principles

There are certain laws that, when followed, lead to a life that flows harmoniously and abundantly. Following these laws leads to living an effective life. Doing the opposite of these laws, lead to feelings of lack and pain. In the section to follow, I have shared some of the Universal Laws that I have found will lead to abundance. One who does not live by Universal Laws is like a ship that never leaves the harbor. Benjamin Franklin logged his ability to follow the laws, or principles as he called them, that he kept each day in a journal and you could do the same.

Below is a starter list of principles, values and meditations to get you on the road to success. I recommend expanding this list as you discover more in your life. By building your own it is an act of self-care as you are practicing self-love.

Express Gratitude: *I am grateful for the gifts God bestows upon me each day.*

Think Vision: *Given that our thoughts dictate our conditions, I will keep only those conditions that I desire in the forefront of my mind and trust in the inspirations that follow.*

Strive for Better: *I will continually strive to increase my vibration by organizing, serving, and making improvements in my current environment.*

Get Rest: *I go to bed when sleepy and wake up at a fixed time every day.*

Practice Success In Business: *I succeed in business by performing my service in an organized, calm, and professional manner. I will always strive for excellence and focus on only one thing at a time as I work through my daily task list.*

Practice Humility: *I am a humble servant of God who realizes inspiration and redirects my course as needed without ego. I perform God's work and I do God's Will each and every day.*

Maintain Integrity: *I mean what I say and I say what I mean. I do all I can to maintain my integrity.*

Be Punctual: *I am on time and respect the time of others. I am where I say I will be.*

Exercise Daily: *I exercise each day. I am so healthy that I MUST workout.*

Enjoy Food: *I practice portion enjoyment through Zen*

eating practices. I enjoy my food by chewing at least 20 times per bite.

Plan Each Day: *I begin each day by creating a prioritized and numbered action list. Do I like making my task list? Not necessarily, but boy does it work!*

Complete All Tasks: *I chain myself to my desk to finish my tasks.*

Concentration of Power: *I maintain concentration of power and make others aware to avoid distraction.*

Express Appreciation: *I appreciate what I already have and regulate my life to what I can do and what I can have in this moment.*

Maintain Good Posture: *I have excellent posture.*

Practice Good Speech: *I speak slowly and distinctly.*

Be Adventurous: *My life is a daring adventure and I am on a search for treasures within my work. I know, that as Mark Victor Hansen says, me setting my goals is me treasure mapping the adventure of my life. I understand and accept that adventure is not always comfortable. One of my mentors once said, "I want to get to my grave holding on for dear life!" God calls on us to begin* adventures, not to rest. For this reason, the word 'retire' should be removed from our vocabulary. As Bob Proctor says, "To retire is to back out of life." The performance of service is the gateway and access path to adventure and freedom.

Find Balance: *I choose to remain balanced and poised.*

Develop Wisdom: *I am a wise person who understands causation. I am accountable for my thoughts and choose to act with truth.*

Uphold Truth. *Truth is a defining cause and therefore it guides my actions.*

Practice Stillness: *Each night I plan for the following day by saying, "Heart, be still. Live now in peace and sleep soundly."*

Energy Releaser: *I manifest life, dreams, and wealth. By having the pressure of clear goals and working on them, I am an ENERGY RELEASER.*

Feel Joyous: *I perform my service with joy and express happiness with a smile.*

Make Time to Reflect: *I regularly schedule at least 15 minutes per day to reflect, meditate, and plan.*

Conscious Unity with God: *My relationship with God is priority #1 and through gratitude, it is awesome.*

Hold Noble Ideals: *I commit to actions and walk paths that lead me to my noblest ideals.*

Be Powerful & Effective: *I am powerful and effective and people enjoy listening to me speak.*

Part IV:
Real-Time Vision
Crystallization

When we wake in the morning, our mind is a blank canvas. To create our day, we paint on this canvas with our thoughts. We can choose to do this ourselves or we can allow others to do it for us…this is up to us. It is important to recognize that anything you have ever accomplished began as a goal or a simple idea. The same is true of the future. Right now, your vision is materializing through complete trust in the Universe, gratitude and action. These next sections are all about action. I highly encourage you do the exercises the first time you go through this and anytime you want to set new goals. Sit down in a quiet place with a pen and paper, turn off your phone and stay in a state of creation.

Acknowledgement of Your Journey: As an exercise, make a list of your past accomplishments, big and small, starting from childhood to adulthood. The following list of questions is only intended to prompt your memory. Some questions may apply and some will not. In the end, your list of accomplishments will be unique.

- Were you ever Student of the Month?
- Did you hold any student government positions?
- Were you a member of any clubs?
- Did you sing or play an instrument?
- Do you speak any languages?
- Do you play any sports or were you a member of a team?
- Are you good at any games?
- Did you graduate from any schools?
- Were you ever in a play? Did you learn the lines?
- Did you have a best friend or a girlfriend/boyfriend?
- Did you ever plan and enjoy a successful vacation?
- Did you ever start a business? Did you learn from the experience(s)?
- Did you have any long-term romantic relationships?
- Did you ever hold a leadership position or run for political office?
- Do you like to read? What are your favorite books?
- Did you ever speak in public?
- Did you ever accomplish a goal by its due date?
- Did you ever write a manuscript or book?

- Did you ever go for a hike, bike ride, or run or walk in a marathon?
- What have you already successfully purchased? Did you ever buy a computer, car, home, sofa, painting, etc.?
- Did you ever paint a painting?

Think of some of the important lessons you have learned on your journey. Think of all of the wonderful things you have done in your life and then take 15 more seconds to *focus on your gratitude for the experience.* Bring your mind to a state where you can visualize and *actually feel* the future and all that you may be adding to your list.

Crystallization of Your Vision

As Wallace Waddles teaches in *The Science of Being Great,* everything starts with thought and this, in turn, dictates our conditions. To crystallize our vision, we must create an image in our mind that is so clear that we FEEL it is true in mind and have gratitude for it.

Brian Tracey's *Goals Program*[xxi] provides certain focal points for visualizing and manifesting our goals into reality. The following points were inspired by this program. Use each point as you mentally create and concentrate on your vision.

- **Frequency**: Practice holding your vision at the forefront of your mind as much as possible throughout the course of your day.
- **Duration**: As you focus on your vision, practice holding it in your mind a little longer each time as if you were building a muscle.
- **Vividness**: Make this mental image as vivid as possible. Fill your senses with the colors, fragrances, and feelings of your vision. Imagine the physical feelings of your vision as true. Think of the peace in your soul, the tastes of the cuisine, touch

the steering wheel of your new car, feel the sun on your face, the tropical breeze on your skin, the cold water as you dive into your pool, the feeling of love in your relationship, the feeling of wealth as you can afford anything you desire.

- **Intensity**: When we concentrate on a thought or mental vision, we can summon powers we did not know even existed. *Think with intensity.* If you want something bad enough, you will perform actions to get it and your vision will materialize faster than you could possibly have imagined. Think of the mother who lifted the car because her child was stuck under it. You can do anything with the right motivation! Do all you can to think of your vision as if it is true, NOW!

- **Gratitude**: You must - *absolutely* must - take mental ownership of your vision. Live and be grateful as if that vision were already true. Mentally and physically, cultivate the seed that will grow into the life that you desire. Believe and be grateful with every bit of your psyche and soul that you are in fact living your vision.

Real Time Vision Crystallization Workshop

Again, if this is your first time doing this workshop, I encourage you to turn off your phone, put a do not disturb note on the door and to get a clean pad of paper and a pen or pencil to start on your vision creation process. In 1964, The Beatles were already wealthy, but Paul McCartney and John Lennon sat down to write a song and said, *"Okay! Today, let's write a swimming pool"* and moments later, the song HELP! was written, and that song earned multiple swimming pools. They said it was great motivation. There is a joke I love, *"Why did the Rockstar bring a pen on stage, he wanted to draw a big crowd"*. Right now, you have the opportunity to create ANYTHING you want and can do so with pen and paper. I have run this goal setting and vision creation workshop for YEARS and have people who wrote down yachts, apartments & penthouses in major cities, cars, businesses, relationships, financial freedom, books, etc, and achieved them!!! The point is that right now, create the life you want on paper. I encourage you to go for whatever you desire and to live, proudly, as that person now. In your vision, if you have private jets, yachts, helicopters and luxury apartments, be proud of them! Be proud of that future and truly feel the jet is fueled up in your hanger. I encourage you to think bigger than you ever have and to be proud of your vision. Never, ever think that having a big vision will somehow put others off. Let your vision inspire others to think bigger! Do not let anyone else's small vision shrink yours, if someone puts down your vision, remember what we discussed earlier about vision hijackers. Some people you can inspire, while others, putting people down is their nature and you must make the choice as to if you want them in your life. Also, remember a well-known fact. If you ask someone who has not done the thing you want to do, they will laugh at you. But when you tell someone who has done what you want to do, they will ask you how you will do it! If you want a Leer Jet, perhaps ask someone who has one how they earned it!

This next section recaps *in real time* the formula for creating a vision that this book has laid out for you. As you work through each of the seven sections, be sure to construct, paint, sculpt, engineer, create, and breathe your vision into your mind and *believe it is already true*. The first step is goal setting, then creating affirmations, then turning these into your vision, then the tools to feel gratitude for your vision. To avoid thinking and writing goals twice, we are breaking down the sections of your goal setting below that we will dive into:

- **Personal**
- **Physical Health**
- **Relationships**
- **Society/Community**
- **Material/Thing**
- **Financial**
- **Business/Service Goals**
- **Peer Group**

If you feel nervous, like you are going to jump out of your skin, you should! What you are about to write WILL be your future! Let's get on with it and create a future that truly inspires you! I am going to read some statements to get your mind turning, take the time you need to really get it all out! As Mark Victor Hansen recommends, *"Write down every good thing you want to be, do or have… Write down your hopes, plans, aspirations and high purposes… "*[xxii] Think of your goals from these time frames: *"whole life, next ten years, next five years, this year, this week, today."*[xxiii] Also, really think of how you want to grow, *"mentally, physically, emotionally, spiritually."*[xxiv] Now, let's get to creating your future!

Personal

The first dimension of goal setting involves our **personal dreams and aspirations**. Please label this section *"Personal Goals."*

Please visualize aspects of the personal realm of your life:

- Do you want to love yourself?
- Do you want to believe in yourself?[xxv]
- Do you want to become a terrific thinker?[xxvi]
- Do you want to take total responsibility for your life?
- Do you want to feel fulfilled and happy?
- Do you want to become an inspired artist?[xxvii]
- What is your spiritual life? Do you want to grow spiritually every day?
- Do you want to love and be loved?
- How much daily time do allot to contemplating where and who you are?
- Do you want to become an effective business executive?
- What books will you read?[xxviii]
- How is your relationship with what you believe to be a higher power, God, Universal Mind, or Infinite Intelligence?

- What courses will you take?[xxix]
- How do you view yourself? Do you love yourself?
- What speakers will you experience?
- Are there skills that you would like to develop? This may include learning a foreign language, public speaking, improving computer or typing skills, learning to dance, paint, or play a musical instrument, improving time management and/or delegation abilities, etc. Perhaps you would like to acquire a trade or go back to school.
- Do you want to write a book or screenplay?
- What music will you listen to?[xxx]
- How do you feed your attitude? In other words, what stimuli do you put into your mind on a daily basis? Do you input positive stimuli such as literature, positive music, and educational audio books? Do you work in a positive environment? Are you avoiding living through other people's lives and mindless distractions such as television, talk radio, video games, and random internet information? What stimuli do you need to perform at your best? What stimuli will heighten your awareness on the future?
- Do you make a good first impression?

- When you meet new people, do you welcome them with new conversation and an open hand? How do people greet you in return?

- Are you charismatic and enthusiastic in your daily demeanor?

- Do you approach every situation with a positive attitude?

- Do you introduce yourself at dinner parties?

- Do you contribute to a charity? If so, which one and why?

- Have you thought of different ways that you could improve yourself and your surroundings at home?

I've provided the above simply to get your mind moving. Some questions may apply and, again, many may not. Your goals are unique to your vision. Use your answers to clarify your personal vision.

The next section focuses on your physical journey that is imperative to maintaining self-esteem, health, and longevity.

Physical Health

We only have one mind and body with which we are blessed. Please label this section *"Physical Health."*

- Are you taking care of your health and body?
- Do you feel that you are using your body in an ideal fashion? If not, do you want to change?
- Are you working out regularly and following an exercise schedule?
- Are you planning your meals or are you eating in a hit or miss fashion?
- What is your desired weight, measurements?[xxxi]
- What diet will you follow to get there?[xxxii]
- When will you go to sleep?
- What will you do during your leisure hours?
- Will you perform adventure cardio on weekends, such as hikes, paddle boarding, skiing, etc.?
- Do you want to bring your body to a physical level that provides the ultimate in performance in all areas of life?
- Do you want to practice martial arts?
- Do you want to look like you always dreamed of looking? Does looking like this add to your confidence and sex appeal?
- Do you want to eat only organic foods?
- Do you want to make and enjoy fresh juice every day?

- All of your physical fitness goals are continual goals. You should schedule at least one hour per day to exercise and showering. You should also schedule at least a half hour per day to preparing the meals you will eat.

Relationships

The next step of goal setting regards your relationships with yourself, God, your significant other, your family, friends, and business associates. Please label this section *"Relationships."*

- Do you spend a few minutes alone each day to reflect, pray and meditate? It has been said that prayer is speaking to God and meditation is listening.
- Who are the people most important to you and how would you like to care for them?
- Do you want to understand others better?[xxxiii]
- Are you a parent, son, brother, sister or friend?
- What would you like to do for your children?
- What do you want to do around the house?
- Do you want to meet a romantic partner? If so, define the person's characteristics in detail.

- What do you want to do to be romantic to your mate?

- What will you do in the time you have with your children?

- Do you want to finance a college education?

- Do you want to go on a family vacation?

- Do you talk with your family at the dinner table?

- Do you request that everyone put their cell phones away at meals so you can all really listen and share with each other?

- Do you want to spend more time with those you love?

- As a son/daughter, do you spend enough time with your parents? Do you want to take them out and tell them that you love them?

- If you have siblings, do you spend quality time together?

- As a friend, do you make an effort to stay in touch on a regular basis?

- Do you want to spend more time with your family and loved ones?

- Do you communicate with your business associates regularly?

- Do you acknowledge people for who they are and how much they do for and mean to you?
- Do you validate and encourage others in your life to set their own goals and live their vision?

Please take ten more seconds to think of any other aspects of your relationships that you can visualize.

Society & Community

The next stage of this visualization exercise asks that you clarify your role and purpose in society. This exercise will also help you to attract abundance in a variety of ways through service. Please label this section *"Society & Community."*

No person is an island. Each of us has a role to play within our family, community, town, county, state, country, world, universe, and beyond. Know, with certainty, that you make a HUGE impact to those in your personal Universe. Know, how important you are and how much you and your actions mean to those in your life. The greatest among us know that to achieve real "greatness", we must serve others. Hence, the phrase "the greatest among us shall serve". Many people mistakenly think greatness occurs when others provide service to us, like being on the VIP line at a club, but this simply is not true. The more that we serve, the more we shall receive. If you have always believed that achieving "greatness" means that others serve *you,* then I ask that you change your paradigm. Authentic "Greatness" comes from serving the community, the people around you, and the customers of your business, which we will discuss in depth below. In order to really live your vision, you have to help others live theirs. This being true, why, then, are we waiting to be great when all we have to do is get to work and provide service? It's an easy fix and a win-win!

There certainly is a time to appreciate the service of others and, yes, most of us are thankful and appreciative to all those who work in food service, hospitality, and other types of businesses. However, if you feel that you are always grateful but still find that your life is lacking then you need to step it up. If your mindset is one of lack, you need to begin overwhelming the world with a unique type of service that only you can provide. If you seek abundance, then you must serve abundantly. Provide service to others worthy of a billion dollars and take only what you need from that to live out your vision. This type of attitude is where the 'or more' comes in at the end of your goals. By overwhelming the World with service, more than you can even imagine comes to you!

A good friend of mine has a life whose example is "serving all you can, in every situation". This friend is a man who lives in a perpetual state of action and service. He can always be found participating in some sort of service to others and will jump up enthusiastically to pitch in whenever he can help, in every situation. As a result, he is wealthy in all aspects of his life. Indeed, abundance is his reward.

How does this work? Let's create your channels of service in your vision!

- In your community, do you give freely of your time and energy?
- Do you feel that you would make a great coach?
- Do you want to run for office?
- Who do you want to meet?[xxxiv] Maybe write them a letter?
- Who do you want to get to know?
- Do you see any opportunities to serve that you may be neglecting now?
- Do you want to have your neighbors over for dinner?

- Do you have any old friends with whom you would like to stay in touch?

- Do you want to host a party and entertain your guests?

Take a few moments to visualize how you will serve others in the coming days. Let your imagination soar to amazing heights and be creative! You may find yourself serving not one but thousands of people!

Material "Thing" Goals

Please label this section *"Material/Thing Goals."* Make no mistake...goals that are purely material are still very important. The goal of setting material goals is to get you into a vibration where you truly feel abundant and that you can have any material thing you choose in your life. Benjamin Franklin once said, *"There are two ways of being happy: We must either diminish our wants or augment our means - either may do. The result of each is the same and the decision to decide which is easier is up to each person."* I personally prefer the latter - that is, to augment our means to get what we want. If you disagree, that is fine. Make your choice. The only permission you need, as Bob Proctor and Joe Vitale teach, is that YOU desire it. You desiring it is your signal that it will be in your life. If anyone has done it, you can do it, too, and more! You don't need anyone's permission either, right now, create the material life you desire.

To help visualize your life in the material realm, ask yourself the following questions:

- Do you desire to live in a dream house, condo or apartment? If so, what does this place look like from the outside and from the inside? Imagine the surrounding landscape and the layout of each and every room.
- Do you want a house by the ocean?[xxxv]
- What will be the location of your new residence? Will it be a major city or the suburbs or out in the country?
- Do you desire to own a yacht or a sailboat? What does each vessel look like?
- What are the foods that you and your family consume in order to be healthy?
- Where is the destination of your next adventure vacation?
- How will you continue your education - through school, books, seminars, home study courses, etc.?

- Do you have a gym membership or a home gym and does either have the equipment needed to ensure that you exercise regularly?
- What kind of transportation do you choose?
- Do you desire to own a private helicopter or jet?
- What would you like to be doing in your free time?
- How does it feel to experience the things you wrote above?

You can take complete mental ownership of your financial vision simply by imagining that your wealth has already occurred (because it has!). Give gratitude and thanks that all your goals are real in this moment. To live this life, let's now discuss your financial and business goals to create the cash flow necessary to realize your vision.

Financial

Please label this section "*Financial.*" These questions are a bit subjective because we need our business/service goals to create the cash flow, but think big and answer them the best you can:

- What type of cash flow do you need to earn the goals you wrote above?
- What kind of savings do you want?

- What is your net worth?

- How much do you want to give/tithe and to what organizations?

Business/Service Goals:

The next aspect of vision creation involves taking the necessary actions to acquire the lifestyle you want. Please label this section *"Business/Service."* What we do to make the cash flow to live our vision is the service we render to civilization. Since we already know that the greatest among us shall serve, let's take this Universal Law a step further. Walter Russell believed in a concept called Life Triumphant. He stated, *"The Life Triumphant is that which places what a man gives to the world in creative expression far ahead of that which he takes from it of the creation of others."* To live the Life Triumphant means to serve the equivalent of an ocean while taking just a drop in return to live your life. Remember, on the universal scale, a mountain is very small. Your vision - as articulated in the previous visualization exercise - is small on this same scale. Your *visionary belief* should be one that makes your vision feel real in the present moment. Think of the size of a mountain as compared to the Milky Way Galaxy. It is small, right? Think of your vision compared to the same scale. You must feel that it is easy for you to manifest your vision from The Universe, because it is small. The fact that someone else has done it proves this! You can do what they did and MORE!! Live each day believing that you already have what you desire and you shall receive.

There is a circuit to life that connects us to God/The Universe and the service we choose to perform. As Wallace Waddles once said, *"God, the One Substance, is trying to live and do and enjoy things through humanity. He is saying, 'I want hands to build wonderful structures, to play divine harmonies, to paint glorious pictures; I want feet to run my errands, eyes to see my beauties, tongues to tell mighty truths and to sing marvelous songs."* The way this circuit works is that we appreciate in direct proportion to our level of service. We cannot appreciate until we serve and we cannot truly enjoy the material aspects of life unless we earn them ourselves.

In regards to the financial side, if you created your business with the two attributes we mentioned before, with monthly recurring income and the ability to delegate the work, you can become financially free. In order to get the material things you wrote, simple put the cash flow in place that pays for the monthly payment of the material thing you want. Then, just run a good business, have stable cash flow and the material things will be simply paid off over time. You can do this process for any material thing, including homes, vacations, educations and anything you can imagine.

- Do you want to own a successful business?[xxxvi]
- How will you make your initial income? Remember Andrew Carnegie's tale of "grim necessity". Our goal with our vision is to determine what we love doing with our time, then to do those things. Initially, learn to love the job you have and pridefully become the best at it. Believe that job is a necessary part of your education and learn all you can from it and the people who surround you. When I worked six jobs, I was in the same state of grim necessity where I had to pay my bills, but learned a tremendous amount from each job and took that to my current business. You may say, "six jobs", that sounds like a lot. No, it was what it took at the time to keep me financially afloat. Remember, to live your vision you must do whatever it takes.
- Do you want to become more efficient?[xxxvii]
- What profession do you visualize? Remember, there are 168 hours in a week out of which 68 should be

free to create and serve after working a 40 hour week and sleep are deducted.

- How will you fulfill your creative visualizations and business goals? Will you need more qualifications and skills? Do you need to redo your resume and cover letter? Are you planning to earn your income through an entrepreneurial venture or an intellectual property or a subscription website?
- What type of venture do you want to start? What is the idea? When are you going to write the business plan? Do you know *how* to write a business plan? Whom do you need to get as part of your team? How will you finance your venture?
- What is your clearest purpose in life? What is your *channel* of service?
- What would be the thing you would do if you didn't have to think about money?
- What are some opportunities you could create in your current business/industry?
- Could you become a consultant doing what you do now, to your current company and do an even better job?
- What are some potential businesses you can start doing such things?

When it comes to service goals, there is no pressure. As you complete version 1.0 of your vision, hold it in mind, and are grateful for it, you will receive inspiration on how to accomplish it. It is up to you to capture those inspirations and to act on them.

Peer Group

Please label this section Peer Group. This section sets the goal of who you will be your frame of reference as you make decisions. If you asked Arnold Schwarzenegger if you should set the goal to get ripped, what do you think he would say? If you asked Leonardo Davinci about your new invention, would he encourage you to start it? If you asked J.K. Rowling if you should pen your new book idea, what do you think she would say? You become the average of your peer group. Now, take a moment to create your peer group. This idea was clearly articulated by Scott Alexander, the author of *Rhinoceros Success*. Scott calls it Rhino Portraits. He says, *"Another good idea is to find pictures of rhinoceroses and hang them in your home to constantly remind you of your proud heritage. The bathroom is a great place. It will give you something to think about while you sit there. Make a new family album. Find a picture of a family of rhinos and claim it as your family. If you can find a poster of a charging rhinoceros, that is excellent! Frame it and hang it in your living room. Look for rhinoceroses carved out of wood at your local animal park. The idea is to constantly remind yourself that you are a powerful, charging rhinoceros. Look out world!"*[xxxviii] If you have not read Rhinoceros Success, get it as a hardcover, audible and Kindle. Read it regularly. I think it is one of the best books ever written and it has, no exaggeration, changed the lives of myself and many of my friends/fellow rhinos!

Your peer group can be anyone, not just rhinoceroses, and they do not have to be alive! Write down all of the people you want to be in your peer group, they could range from historical figures, to friends and family. Do you want Ben Franklin, Mother Teresa, Leonardo Davinci, William Shakespeare, Arnold Schwarzenegger Michelangelo, Dr. Martin Luther King, Jr., any business leaders, athletes, authors, speakers, etc., take a moment to write down anyone you can think of whom you want to be a part of your peer group. As you think, think of bumping your ideas off of your peer group and what they would say to your vision and inspirations. They would ask, sounds awesome, how do you plan to do it?! When you look at the photos of your peer group, imagine yourself doing that they did, multiplied and with the creative application of your unique talents, skills, personality and abilities. You can do what they did, multiplied, exponentially. Just one example, there are now more phones on the planet than people. Think about that. If you develop a product delivered to phones and were able to deliver to a portion of those users, it would make you wealthy financially. There is more opportunity now than ever!!

I hope you physically sat down to write out your goals on paper, if you just read or listened to this as a refresher, that is great, too. Now, I want you to number each of your goals, by section, in order of their importance. I want you to go through personal, number your goals, 1, 2, 3, etc. Then to physical and number those 1, 2, 3 etc. Do that for all seven sections.

Creating Affirmations from Your Goals

Okay, now that you have a prioritized lists of goals, we are going to turn them into affirmations. An affirmation is the act of confirming something to be true. This is a key to this entire process, to believe that the goals you set are true now and to have gratitude for them presently. Now, I want you to take the top two goals from each section, that will equal 14 goals total. I want you to write those goals out on a separate piece of paper and write them with the *Triple P Principle*, as invented by Brian Tracey, as instructed below, to your goals.

As Brian Tracy explains, the Triple P Principle transforms your goals into a list of affirmations that you can read, re-read, and re-write. The Triple P has three Parts:

1. **Present**: Write your affirmation in the present tense (e.g. I have, I own, I am, I speak, etc.)
2. **Personal**: Write your affirmation in the personal tense. As Brian Tracy says, "You are the only person in the Universe who can say 'I' in relation to *you*." (e.g. I have, I own, I am, etc.)
3. **Positive tense**: Write your affirmation in the positive tense. Only use words that express

positively what you want in your life *today*. For example, the use of the word "don't" in the affirmation "I don't eat fast food" reflects what you *don't* want. Instead, say, "I will only put food and drink in my body that is conducive to perfect health".

We are going to add two more sections to this process:

4. **Add the Phrase "Or Better" as Joe Vitale recommends**: Or better, leaves your mind open for the Universe to provide even more to you than you even imagined. This also leaves open your faith that the goal may not come in a form or way that you expected, but by writing this, you have trust that the best outcome will happen, no matter the journey to get there.

5. **Due Date**: As Brian Tracy recommends, give each of your goals a due date. A due date is very important and is the exclamation point on the affirmation! Each goal's due date holds you accountable to a task's completion and, thus, motivates you to get out of bed and complete it. Remember, this is the same concept as working out in the gym. You are not competing against anyone

but yourself and the number of reps completed or the time you achieved last week. The same principle applies to goal setting. You are exactly where you are supposed to be but by setting a due date, you push yourself to meet the date you set. The only competition you have in life, at all, is the person staring back at you in the mirror.

Committing to Your Vision

I borrowed this part from Tony Robbin's Goal Setting Workshop. Please, take a moment to write out your goal and write a short paragraph as to WHY you must accomplish it. This will cement the reasons why creating this life and doing the required work is absolutely necessary. Please take a moment to do this for each of your affirmations.

Etching Your Vision into Your Subconscious, Raising Your Subconscious Vibration

The entire goal of all of the above exercises is to convince your subconscious mind into believing that you already live your vision. The process of subconscious vibration is what Denis Waitley describes as *Visual Motor Rehearsal*. This process gets your subconscious to vibrate at a level where you are the person who has earned the life you wrote above. Your subconscious will vibrate at whatever frequency your conscious mind tells it to. As Bob Proctor says in is book, *The Art of Living*, "*When you build an image in your mind of what you want, you've got to understand that your subconscious mind cannot reject it. It (your subconscious mind) is totally subjective. 100%. And it cannot differentiate between what is real and what is imagined. It must accept it.*" He then goes onto say, "*What I just covered there is the most important thing you could ever learn.*"[xxxix] For Bob Proctor to say this is the most important thing you could ever learn is pretty significant. What he means by this is all you have to do is continually hold the image of what you want, aka, your vision, and your subconscious mind will accept it as the truth and will vibrate at whatever frequency you chose to make your vision. If your vision requires a car, you will vibrate at that frequency, if your vision requires a relationship, you will vibrate at that frequency, if your vision requires a private jet, you will vibrate at that frequency.

The next few steps will help you hold your vision and further etch it into your subconscious. I am sure you heard the concept of a vision board. A vision board is a tool that your goals/affirmations can be turned into in order to make your vision crystal-clear. Your mind communicates to Universal Mind through images and your mind can only hold one image at a time. As you think, having the photos available in your head makes it so much clearer. Remember what Anthony Robbins says, *"Clarity is Power!"* The clearer the image you hold in your mind, your vision, the more clearly, powerfully, intensely and specifically it is communicated to The Universe. Also, remember what Joe Vitale recommends, that our vision is just the idea we are conveying. The life conditions we receive may be different and BETTER than the exact vision we are communicating. This is why we say, or better, at the end of our affirmations.

Our goal with this next section is to download 5 to 15 photos of each section of your goals/affirmations and turn each of the seven sections you defined into 8.5 x 11 inch future tiles that you can print on a color printer and hang up in your home or office. A future tile is a printed collage of photos that represent a specific goal. For example, if you want a new Corvette. Create a future tile of various photos of that new Corvette to prompt you to imaging driving and experiencing it. I recommend doing this same process for all of your goals. Perhaps you have heard the concept of a vision board, from amazing movie *The Secret*, by Rhonda Byrne. When you first hear the idea, you may question its effectiveness, but it really works. Your mind works through images and having this tool to see your future through images that you specifically chose and organized, then to see yourself *through* them, is just so powerful. Also, if you really, truly want the life of your vision, I recommend having the attitude, "*Whatever it takes!*" If the process of creating a vision board accelerates your vision manifestation at all, isn't it worth it? I originally called these vision tiles, but then, one day when I was creating one of a new condo in Florida for my wife and I, I said to my wife, "*Honey, let's create that future tile of our place in Florida.*" When I said future tile, I was like, *that is it*, that is what it is, it is a visual representation of our future. I recommend hanging these future tiles on your refrigerator, in your home gym, or on any open wall that you have that you want to be a reminder of how frigging awesome your future is!

Now, comes the fun part! Carve out about an hour of time, trust me, this is the most important part of the process of future creation. You can now download photos of each section of your goals and make them into your future/vision board(s)! You can call it whatever you want, vision board or future board, but the key is you know that whatever you have in those pictures will absolutely be your future. Here is what you do:

    1.   On your local computer, create a folder called VisionBoard or FutureBoard, whichever you like more.

    2.   In that folder, create sub folders for each section of your vision:

        a. Personal

        b. Physical Health

        c. Relationships

        d. Society_Community

e. Material_Thing

f. Financial

g. Business_Service

h. Peer_Group

3. Then, go to the online and download photos that inspire you for each section and download them into the appropriate folder. I recommend, 5-15 photos for each section.

4. Then, the FUN part starts. The next step is the best! We are going to transform your photos into 8.5 x 11 inch collages for each individual part of your vision. To do this please go to: *turbocollage.com.* I know, it sounds like Arnold Schwarzenegger named this software!

5. This software is the BEST collage making software I have ever seen. I manually created my first good vision board into 8.5 x 11 inch future tiles in Photoshop and it took me over six hours to make them! This software does them almost instantaneously. The reason the 8.5 x 11 inch size is so important is that you

can print them right off of your local printer and make as more than one copy for yourself! You may want to print more out so you can hang your future tiles in your bathroom, on your refrigerator and anywhere else you want to see your vision. There is a free version of Turbo Collage that produces a watermark on the finished work. To get the watermark off, you need to purchase it. If you are making collages for personal use, it is $14.99/year. That is a bargain! I would just buy it! This software is worth its weight in gold!

6. You are going to want to do a separate future tile for each section of your goals. From here, you literally:

    a. Open the software

    b. Open the folder relating to the future tile you are creating, e.g. personal

    c. Drag your images into the pictures section

    d. Then go to settings

e. Choose your size, I recommend 8.5x11 so you can easily print them right to your printer

f. Choose the pattern you like, I love the Zig Mosaic

g. You can play with the position of each photo to focus on what you want to focus on, you can rearrange the photos, add text and much more

h. I would save the layout by going file save and save the Turbo Collage project so you can edit your future tiles as you accomplish your goals

i. From there, you simply press export, then export as a JPG, then save it with the appropriate name, such as: VisionTilePersonal, VisionTileBusiness, etc.

j. Then, you simply print out the collages or Future Tiles that you just created for each section and hang them on your refrigerator, your vision board, your home gym, or wherever you have open space!

How cool is this!!! Now, you have your vision. What you see on your Vision Board that you created IS your future. Now, when you think. THINK your vision board! THINK as the person who has that entire vision board in your life NOW! Literally, put yourself into the photos and visualize yourself doing exactly what you see on the board. Your eyes are the eyes of the person looking out at you! Have gratitude for everything you are experiencing. When you are driving, consciously think of your vision. When you are in the shower, think of your vision. When you are working out, think of your vision. Mentally, go tile by tile and feel gratitude for all that exists in that vision. FEEL it the leather steering wheel, breath in the warm tropical air, feel ripped and in the best shape of your life, walk on a hike with your significant other, FEEL & EXPERIENCE your entire vision, then just close your eyes, point your head toward the sky and say THANK YOU! Make your thoughts your vision and feel GRATITUDE for your entire vision.

The goal is to become the person in your subconscious mind who has this life now. The job of your conscious mind is to think it with these tools, then your subconscious must vibrate on a level where you truly feel as if that life is yours. Having that life means that your life is AWESOME and exactly where you want it to be. This is the goal of the entire vision creation process. The goal of the entire process is to create your goals, turn them into a vision, then gratefully THINK that vision as true right now.

This is a POWERFUL process and one that will change your life if you take the time to simply do it. I consider a goal setting, vision creation workshop as a massage for your mind and soul. You are creating thoughts you LOVE and thoughts that truly inspire YOU, not thoughts placed in your mind by others.

A second way I recommend to etch your goals into your subconscious mind is to experience them as much as possible. If you have a car that you want, go for a test drive, or better yet, rent it for a few days. If you have a vacation home you would like to buy, AirBNB it for a week and feel how it feels to live there. If you want a relationship, go out immediately and put yourself in a situation where you could meet someone. Get out there and do whatever you can to experience your goal, TODAY!

The third way I recommend to carve your goals onto your subconscious mind is to get physical visual reminders.

This really applies to your peer group and art in general. Get paintings, busts and sculptures of the people you want in your peer group. Go on Amazon and eBay and find some sculptures, paintings, etc., you like and buy them. Then, place them throughout your home and office. Art and interior design also have ways of attracting more beauty in your life, too. Having and appreciating art is a form of gratitude and brings more of the best and most beautiful things and people into your life. Interior design is a form of art and if you have space, make it beautiful. All you need is to do is make a quick trip to the hardware store to buy some paints, tape and brushes. Then, add some of the artwork and busts as we discussed above. Think of how valuable a small, studio apartment is in a major city near you. If you had that, you would make it beautiful, right? Make your current space in which you live equally as beautiful, by doing so, you show gratitude for what you have and will attract more in the near future.

A fourth way to etch your goals onto your subconscious mind is to re-write them each day and imagine them as you do. Brian Tracy recommends this as do many other people who understand these Universal Laws. *"According to a recent study in a forthcoming issue of the journal Psychological Science, using pen and paper, not laptops, to take notes boosts memory and the ability to retain and understand concepts.*"[xl] Something happens when you re-write ideas and tasks. This process improves your memory and the freshness on your mind. Rewriting the life you want is actually a motivational experience, a method for living our vision in the present and a gift we give ourselves each time we write them down. We literally live our vision in the present moment. It takes less than 5 minutes to write (or re-write) a list of affirmations/goals. I ask the audience to rewrite their affirmations in my goal setting workshop. There has never been a person who goes over five minutes. The average is around two and a half minutes to rewrite a list of affirmations. Try to do this twice per day – when you get up and when you go to bed - to solidify your vision in your subconscious further.

Rewriting your goals, looking at your pictures and experiencing them through, FDVIG, Frequency, Duration, Vividness, Intensity and Gratitude as we discussed before, will ensure that you vibrate on the same frequency as your vision. As you vibrate on your vision frequency and work on your goals, you will receive inspirations. Write your inspirations, add them as goals, create affirmations and add them to your vision. Over time, you will see each goal begin to manifest and as each one completes, remove it from your list and add it to a list of your accomplishments. As you reach your goals, take the time to reset new goals, then download new photos and replace that tile on your vision board. As you do this, your vision will be refined and and your faith and mental ownership will become even stronger because you know this works! This process removes the stress of life as you are certain your vision is your future. Having a clear vision to walk toward allows you to view challenges as stepping-stones. People who are stressed do not have a clear vision in mind and do not work towards goals productively. This transformation occurs because you are clear on your vision and working on goals that you created.

The next part of the process is taking action! Taking action is actually the easy part. Our schooling taught us how to take daily action to learn the material we needed to learn to pass our tests. The only difference now is that it is YOU who created YOUR syllabus. As you are thinking your vision, when inspiration is given to you, take action on it! The idea may apply to your existing business, or it may require you to develop new skills, if it requires new skills, set a goal to learn those skills!

How to Organize and Take Action on Your Goals

How do you create a plan and take action on your goals? Again, this is actually very simple and all it requires is for you to understand the $25,000 Idea[xli] from Earl Nightingale's <u>*Lead The Field Program*</u>. In the hey-day of Carnegie Steel, Andrew Carnegie asked a consultant, Ivy Lee, to visit his offices. He told Lee that '*He went on to tell Ivy Lee that what was needed wasn't more knowing but a lot more doing. He said, "We know what we should be doing. Now if you can show us a better way of getting it done, I'll listen to you and pay you anything within reason you ask."* Lee told Carnegie to take out a piece of paper and write down the six most important things he needed to do tomorrow, then to number them from one to six in order of their importance. Then, he instructed Carnegie to take out the piece of paper upon his arrival in the morning and start work on number one. If something or someone should force its delay, simply move onto number two. Then, when the person or thing that forced number one's delay arrives, go back to number one and complete the task. When number one is completed, you move onto number two. You simply keep moving down the numbered tasks until all are completed. Lee told Carnegie to create this prioritized task list every day and execute each item in order of importance. A few months after this meeting, Ivy Lee received a check in the mail for $25,000 along with a note from Carnegie. In his note, Mr. Carnegie stated that, *"From a financial standpoint, the lesson taught to him by Mr. Lee was the most valuable lesson he had ever learned"* and to accept the money as a small token of his appreciation. Although larger projects may require a more detailed plan, the same process can and should apply.

One's daily planning method is one of the most personal things in a person's life. I recommend using whatever tools you enjoy to plan your day. If you have a certain pen, journal, or paper, use them! Please allow me to tell you what I have found to be effective. First, just as we can only think one thought at a time, we can only do one task at a time. There is no such thing as multitasking. In each moment, we are doing one thing. Number your list, starting with 1, then 2, then 3, and keep going until each task is numbered. You have to have a way to only do one thing at a time, so don't say, A1, A2, B1, B2, just make the list and complete as much as you can each day. Do this and you will see results that you can't imagine. Focus only on the task at hand and give it all you got. Don't believe it can be this simple? Listen to what Andrew Carnegie, literally, the riches self-made person in history thought of this method. Earl Nightingale writes, *"The entire interview hadn't taken more than a half-hour. In a few weeks the story has it that the company president sent Ivy Lee a check for $25,000 with a letter saying the lesson was the most profitable, from a money standpoint, he'd ever learned in his life. And it was later said that in five years this was the plan that was largely responsible for turning what was then a little-known steel company into one of the biggest independent steel producers in the world. One idea, the idea of taking things one at a time in their proper order. Of staying with one task until it's successfully completed before going on to the next."[xlii]* Trust me. Just make a list, in whatever form you like, using whatever tools you like, then number that list from 1 to the end. Then, get to number one and finish it, then number 2, etc., and you will see results that you can't believe.

I encourage you to read *Essentialism, The Disciplined Pursuit of Less* by Greg McKeown. In his book, he says we can either go a millimeter in a million directions or go big in one direction. If you want to see your vision manifested, I encourage you to apply the $25,000 rule and focus on a specific goal until it is done. This being said, you will often, as I do, have client/work goals and your personal goals and wonder how to delineate between the two. This is what I do. I do customer work from 9am – 5pm and work on my personal goals before 9 and after 5. If I finish my client work between 9 and 5, I have the privilege of getting back to my goals and can work on them during work hours. I say privilege, because, that is how it feels to have a clear goal on which you can't wait to get back to working.

Your main list of goals that you made in the preceding pages should have due dates on them. I recommend that you have a calendar of those due dates and look at it at least every week. Also, as you re-write your goals, re-write the due date and visualize it's accomplishment on that date. This can be considered more of long-term planning. If those goals are in the next 20 years, 10 years, five years or one year, put them on a list and in your calendar with their due date. Look at your long-range goals at least once per week and use the tools above to etch them into your mind. Tacitly speaking on actually getting goals done, this is what I do and recommend.

Creating Your Daily Task List

As soon as you sit at your desk, if you haven't already, I recommend, rewriting your goals for 2-3 minutes. Really visualize that future you created! The power of writing things on paper, *pen-to-paper*, is well documented and you can do a quick internet search to see the effectiveness of it. Once you re-write your goals, get a clean piece of paper out each day. I recommend creating a new list each day as trying to use yesterday's list just doesn't motivate you. It is like drinking yesterday's coffee versus a fresh cappuccino. Creating it fresh gets all the tasks to which you will apply yourself right on the forefront of your mind and gives you a new creation that you can cross out. Re-writing your list gets the cobwebs out of your mind and gets the gears turning in a way that is hard to describe, but really works. Your daily task list is your road map to your vision. Looking at yesterday's list is just unmotivating and does not work. I use a blank piece of my company letterhead each day. Just as rewriting your goals each day improves memory and gives you the ability to live your vision in the present, re-writing your prioritized daily action task list each day gives you a birds eye view of where you are going that day. Think of it like this, have you ever put your destination in a GPS and followed it blindly? You didn't know where you were, what part of the state you were in or even if you were going North or South, right? Isn't it so much better to look at your destination on a map, then in mind, know the direction you are going and the roads you will be taking? This is what creating your list daily does for you. It gives you that higher level summary of what you need to get done and pushes you to get through your tasks focused and efficiently so you can finish your list and do the things on your own list, e.g. coach a team, spend time with your family, workout, go to open mic night, work on writing a book, etc. I highly encourage you to spend the time you need to plan your day. Brian Tracy once said that, *"Every minute you spend in planning saves ten minutes in execution."* This is absolutely true! You may think that re-writing all of your follow up calls from yesterday would be taxing. It is not. When you re-write them, you will visualize a successful outcome and do better on that call, on that email, in that meeting, or on that writing task, etc.

From there, date the top of the page and write a daily affirmation of how you feel right now and your intention for the day. For example, *"I will give each task of this day my full attention and pure power."* From there, below that, write a few columns, I label mine: Delegation, Calls, Emails, Short (meaning tasks that are longer than sending emails, like sending a thank you card or writing a campaign piece for a client), Project, and on the right, I put one called Follow Up. When a task requires me to follow up, for example, I called and got someone's voicemail and want to call them back, I would put that in follow up. On the bottom half of the page, I label that Personal. I put the same exact columns for that section, too. I take out my task list from the day before and review the follow up columns. I write any tasks that have to get done in the appropriate column above, e.g. delegate (tasks to be delegated to my team or vendors), phone calls, emails, short, projects, follow up. From there, I create two separate numbering systems. One for client work and one for my personal goals. I start with delegation and move to the right, through the columns, say there are 15 items to be delegated, they would be labelled 1-15, say twenty phone calls needed to be made, they would be labeled 16-35. Then, I go to the email column, say there are 25 emails to be sent, they would be labeled 36-60, then, say there are 5 short tasks to be done, they would be labeled 61-65. All items are crossed out as they are completed, which feels amazing, and if follow up is necessary, added to the follow-up column. Then, my personal goals are at the bottom of the sheet, which have their own task list of the same exact numbered structure. So, all of my personal goals have the same exact types of steps, delegate, calls, emails, short, projects, follow-up and are numbered separately from one through however many there are. The reason why is that personal goals are only worked on before 9 and after 5 or when customer work is completed.

Then, I say a prayer, thanking God for the ability to do the service before me and pray for a successful day. Usually, it is early in the morning, around 6, so I get to work right away on my personal number 1 goal until it is done, then number 2 until it is done, etc. until 9am. Then, I get to work on client goal number 1 and crank them out until the entire list is complete. There are bankers in New York City who make 400+ phone calls in a day. When I did corporate sales, we had to make 100 calls by 11am. A part of the phone calls we make are through our CRM (customer relationship management) tool that gives us the calls to do that day for an individual lead, prospect or client campaign. I consider CRM calls to be customer related work so it goes in the 9-5 customer/business time zone. When you have the numbered list, something magical happens and you can't wait to get through your calls so you can see a completed list and get to your own, personal goals. Then, when you finish your client list or it hits 5pm, you have the privilege to work on your own, personal numbered list of tasks. This is all you have to do. It is very simple. You just chunk your tasks into the different categories, metaphorically, floor the accelerator for each category, then shift gears into the next category, until your work is completed. As you complete your goals, I encourage you to use the same process in the preceding pages to reset new and bigger goals!

Also, it is okay to NOT do things NOT on your list. To say it properly, it is okay to only perform activities on your list! That means if someone calls to go to lunch and you are jamming, you can say no. What I usually do is chunk my in-person meetings and conference calls into a few days a week, usually, Thursday and Friday. This way, on the days I am at my desk, I am really cranking on my lists; getting my highest priority goals accomplished and actually making progress toward my vision. I am not a huge fan of grabbing lunch during the day either. Remember, when you work, you work, when you play, you play, and don't confuse the two. If I want to see a friend, I think seeing that person after the work day is best so you can actually have no pressure on time and a quality conversation. Now that I am married and have a family, I notice myself calling friends to catch up as I drive.

A big question people ask is how to handle email. I consider email a part of delegation. I check my email at the start of my task list when at my delegation column. It takes me about 20-30 minutes usually to get through my emails and delegate appropriately. Then, I check email again when I get to my email column. Then, if there is something urgent and a client tells me that they need or sent me something via email, I will check it. We have a support email for our company that our team checks regularly, but for me personally, I really put a concerted effort into working on my numbered task at hand. I answer the phone during the business day when at my desk, but really try to get right to the heart of the matter quickly, so I can get the client request handled or delegated appropriately. For these types of tasks, I have a rule I read once. If the 'emergency' takes less than two minutes, I do it immediately, if it takes more than two minutes, I either delegate it or add it to my follow up list to be added to the appropriate column and numbered for the next business day.

This is one way to plan your business day. Again, your preference on your structure is extremely personal, but I hope you find my method somewhat helpful. They key is that you create a list, and number it, then only focus on the number on which you are working until it is done with all the excellence you can muster. If you do a system like this, I guarantee, each day you will accomplish so much, that you will be amazed. Also, during your business day, keep in mind your realized vision and feel gratitude for it. Remember that the tasks on which you are working are creating your realized vision. Your vision is the fuel to get your work done. Keep in mind the words of Earl Nightingale who said, *"Success is the progressive realization of a goal."* As you work on your goals, you are the epitome of success. Remember, the busboy with a clear vision and working on his goals is equally as successful as when he is the restauranteur. As Mark Victor Hansen reminds us in his awesome book, Future Diary, "JC Penny once said, *"Give me a stock clerk with a goal, and I will give you a stock clerk who makes history.""*[xliii] Once you become committed to your goals, you can transform your life so drastically, it will startle you.

This feeling of success is attainable to human beings only when the human being is in active pursuit of a goal. Remember The Beatles? Their music catalog is a timeless treasure. Just like Joe Vitale, where each of his books could be the best book ever written, each song The Beatles produced could be the best song ever made. It is not by chance, however, The Beatles were at the studio at 10am and left after 6pm each day when they were together. They were extremely focused and worked very hard to create what the music they did. The goal of the independence we discuss in this book is not to wake up and watch TV, but to have the time and space freedom to serve where and how you want, but to still have the discipline to apply yourself over periods of time. Personally, I have a rule that I work from 9-5 each day and do not deviate from that schedule. I do not take personal time, break free at 3 in the afternoon, or take days of the week off. I do this because, yes, I truly love what I do, but as an entrepreneur, you must have the daily work ethic to actually create and produce something with your time.

Don't be an entrepreneur in name only, meaning that you are unemployed. The key to being in business is cash flow, and if your business doesn't make the money to pay your bills, work as many jobs as you have to so you can live, but leave the hours you need to serve your clients open so you can run your business. This is exactly what I did. As your business cash flow increases, you spend more time on your business. The key is that you have a structured goal accomplishment system that you employ daily and actually get high demand tasks done as an individual and as an organization.

Then, when you do have time off, at nights and weekends, you truly enjoy it. Again, the old phrase work-hard, play-hard, is completely accurate. I take that phrase to mean, when you work, you work, when you play, you play, and you don't confuse the two. The funny part is that I love what I do so much, that I get up early on Saturday and Sunday to get to my desk and write and work on projects before everyone gets up. The reason why is that I constantly expand my vision by creating big goals and meet them regularly. Big goals, a gratefully clear vision, a prioritized task list, truly looking forward to working on them, then opening your eyes, clapping your hands and jumping out of bed to work on them, keeps you sharp, motivated and youthful. I really believe that thinking bigger is better thinking because bigger thoughts motivate. Bigger, fun thoughts draw you forward through the uncomfortableness to reach them. Thinking bigger truly compels you to go through your own personal evolution on a day-to-day basis. The tools you learned in this book to have a big vision will help you think bigger, and thus better, only filling your mind with thoughts you want to have, that motivate you toward the future you eagerly want to create. Through this system of connecting to The Universe through gratitude for your vision and having the channel of service to bring it to reality, you will experience genius. It is the same exact process that any genius in history took and experienced. Believe you are a genius! If you still have doubts about your inner genius, here is what Marianne Williamson has to say:

Our Greatest Fear by Marianne Williamson

It is our light not our darkness that most frightens us.

Our deepest fear is not that we are inadequate.

Our deepest fear is that we are powerful beyond measure.

We ask ourselves, who am I to be brilliant, gorgeous, talented and fabulous?

Actually, who are you not to be?

You are a child of God.

Your playing small does not serve the world.

There's nothing enlightened about shrinking so that other people won't feel insecure around you.

We were born to make manifest the glory of God that is within us.

It's not just in some of us; it's in everyone.

And as we let our own light shine, we unconsciously give other people permission to do the same.

As we are liberated from our own fear, our presence automatically liberates others.

Know that the best that we can do in this world is to live a great life. Real leadership is accomplished by action. Look to your life and life conditions to motivate and inspire you. When you see someone living a great life, ask this person how he or she did it and then follow suit. Emulate the thinking, philosophies, and habits of those whom you admire. You may find that many of the principles in this book are the same Universal Laws that helped to get them where they are today.

Conclusion

Wallace Waddles once wrote that the innate feeling we have as human beings to *"do more, be more, have more"* is the same feeling that caused a brave fish to crawl on dry land for food. That feeling inside of you - the happy discontent - is divine unrest and the urge of God pushing you forward. Evolution is the excess of life. That yearning for more life through appreciation and enjoyment of the finest experiences and relationships and by the exploration of your mind and creation of new things is God wanting to express himself further through you. Use the powerful force of divine expansion to stretch your comfort zone and become a tool of divine expression to serve more and to become an example to others. The best we can do is become an example of *how to be great* and to *teach others how they, too, can learn to serve and lead great lives.*

Imagine the size of The Universe and the enormous number of stars contained within. In terms of size, Earth is just a small planet circling around and we are mere pebbles on a beach. Viewing life from this vantage point provides us a boost of courage to just *"go for it"*. Despite our size, however, our work is very important, and I encourage you to do all you can to live your vision. The Universe is One and you are a part of it. You are made of the same substance as the Sun and the stars. You need to continually put pressure on yourself through goals to create that fusion reaction to release the best energies possible through service, just like a star. The same massive pressure will create huge diamonds materially for you to enjoy and appreciate. The more focused pressure, the more energy you will experience in your life and the finer material experiences.

Believe that you can do anything! Set a goal, create a vision, take action and *just do it.* Remember the line Patricia (Meg Ryan) says from the motion picture, *Joe Versus the Volcano, "My father says almost the whole world's asleep. Everybody you know, everybody you see, everybody you talk to. He says only a few people are awake. And they live in a state of constant total amazement."*xliv I encourage you to do the exercises in this book to wake up! I ask that you just trust me to set your goals, turn them into affirmations, put due dates on them, say, or better at the end. Then transform each goal into its own future tile, print them and hang those tiles in places where you will see them. As you look at them, visualize yourself *doing* those things and *being* that person. Breathe deep and *imagine* that life as true now! *BELIEVE* it in

GRATITUDE and *BECOME* that person in this moment. This step is *THINKING* as that person. Then, *SPEAKING* as that person. Then, taking *ACTION* on the ideas that cross your mind as that person. Truly feel and believe, in every ounce of your soul, that you are the person in your vision and in no time at all, your *LIFE WILL BE YOUR VISION*. This I promise you and you, too, will live in a state of *constant and total amazement*! Go now, SET BIG GOALS, HOLD A BIG VISION GRATEFULLY IN MIND, LISTEN FOR INSPIRATION and TAKE MASSIVE ACTION EACH DAY to LIVE YOUR VISION!

Apollinaire once said, *"Come to the edge"* and they replied, *"We are afraid"*. *"Come to the edge"*, he said again and this time they came. *"He pushed them and they flew."* You are standing at the edge. Trust me, you can do it. Go forth and fly!

About the Author

Thomas Matthew Roman is the founder and CEO of Roman Media LLC. He has a passion for learning new things and creating cool stuff. Tom loves spending time with his wife and daughter, his work, reading, fishing, watching movies, working out and enjoying life. He is grateful to God, his family, friends, clients and teachers for all they have taught and done for him. He truly tries to live the idea of "If it ain't fun, don't do it!" in every moment of his life. To contact Tom, please visit RomanMedia.com.

A Final Note:

I don't think it is by chance that this book turned out to be exactly 300 pages. It was not planned and when finishing the table of contents, I was like, wow, exactly 300 pages!? One of my favorite movies is *300*, about King Leonidas. I encourage you to watch this movie and when you think of your vision, do so with the same commitment and passion that King Leonidas had. I encourage you to wake up and say, LIVE MY VISION, just like he yells, THIS IS SPARTA! Live deliberately and tie this same intensity and commitment to your vision, speech and actions and your life will become an exact reflection of your vision.

Bibliography

[i] Dooley, Mike. "The Universe Newsletter." TUT, 2019, www.tut.com/.

[ii] Proctor B. Art of Living [Internet]. TarcherPerigee; 2015. 240 p. Available from: https://www.goodreads.com/book/show/25310606-the-art-of-living

[iii] The Edge (Motion Picture: 1997: Tamahori)

[iv] Chandler, 100 Ways to Motivate Yourself, Third Edition: Change Your Life Forever.

[v] Hobbs C. Time Power: The Internationally Acclaimed Insight On Time Management System. The Charles R. Hobbs Corporation; 1987.

[vi] Kiyosaki R. Rich Dad, Poor Dad: What the Rich Teach Their Kids About Money--That the Poor and the Middle Class Do Not! Warner Books Ed; 2009.

[vii] Chandler, 100 Ways to Motivate Yourself, Third Edition: Change Your Life Forever.

[viii] Abbott E. Flatland: A Romance of Many Dimensions. Dover; 1992.

[ix] Canfield J, Victor Hansen M, Hewitt L. The Power of Focus: What the World's Greatest Achievers Know about The Secret to Financial Freedom & Success. Simon & Schuster; 2000.

[x] Canfield J, Victor Hansen M, Hewitt L. The Power of Focus: What the World's Greatest Achievers Know about The Secret to Financial Freedom & Success. Simon & Schuster; 2000.

[xi] "Point of No Return." Wikipedia, Wikimedia Foundation, 19 Nov. 2019, en.m.wikipedia.org/wiki/Point_of_no_return.

[xii] Brenoff, Ann. "Early Retirement May Be The Kiss Of Death, Study Finds." HuffPost, HuffPost, 28 Apr. 2016, www.huffpost.com/entry/early-retirement-may-be-the-kiss-of-death-study-finds_n_57221aa3e4b01a5ebde49eff.

[xiii] "Shark Tank." Spirko, Craig, director. Shark Tank, season 6, episode 25.

[xiv] Paul. Why Was School Created? [Internet]. Available from: https://www.wonderopolis.org/wonder/why-was-school-created

[xv] Shanley, J. P., Hanks, T., Ryan, M., & Bridges, L. (2002). Joe Versus the Volcano. Widescreen. Burbank, CA: Warner Home Video.

[xvi] Hansen, Mark Victor., et al. Future Diary. Mark Victor Hansen Pub. Co., 1989.

[xvii] Hansen, Mark Victor., et al. Future Diary. Mark Victor Hansen Pub.

Co., 1989.

xviii Klein C. 8 Things You May Not Know About the Real Colonel Sanders [Internet]. Available from: https://www.history.com/news/8-facts-real-colonel-sanders-kfc

xix Byrne R. The Secret. Atria Books Beyond Words Publishing; 2006.

xx Hansen, Mark Victor., et al. Future Diary. Mark Victor Hansen Pub. Co., 1989.

xxi Tracy, Brian. Goals: How to Get Everything You Want-- Faster than You Ever Thought Possible. Berrett-Koehler Publishers, 2010.

xxii Hansen, Mark Victor., et al. Future Diary. Mark Victor Hansen Pub. Co., 1989.

xxiii Hansen, Mark Victor., et al. Future Diary. Mark Victor Hansen Pub. Co., 1989.

xxiv Hansen, Mark Victor., et al. Future Diary. Mark Victor Hansen Pub. Co., 1989.

xxv Hansen, Mark Victor., et al. Future Diary. Mark Victor Hansen Pub. Co., 1989.

xxvi Hansen, Mark Victor., et al. Future Diary. Mark Victor Hansen Pub. Co., 1989.

xxvii Hansen, Mark Victor., et al. Future Diary. Mark Victor Hansen Pub. Co., 1989.

xxviii Hansen, Mark Victor., et al. Future Diary. Mark Victor Hansen Pub. Co., 1989.

xxix Hansen, Mark Victor., et al. Future Diary. Mark Victor Hansen Pub. Co., 1989.

xxx Hansen, Mark Victor., et al. Future Diary. Mark Victor Hansen Pub. Co., 1989.

xxxi Hansen, Mark Victor., et al. Future Diary. Mark Victor Hansen Pub. Co., 1989.

xxxii Hansen, Mark Victor., et al. Future Diary. Mark Victor Hansen Pub. Co., 1989.

xxxiii Hansen, Mark Victor., et al. Future Diary. Mark Victor Hansen Pub. Co., 1989.

xxxiv Hansen, Mark Victor., et al. Future Diary. Mark Victor Hansen Pub. Co., 1989.

xxxv Hansen, Mark Victor., et al. Future Diary. Mark Victor Hansen Pub. Co., 1989.

xxxvi Hansen, Mark Victor., et al. Future Diary. Mark Victor Hansen Pub. Co., 1989.

xxxvii Hansen, Mark Victor., et al. Future Diary. Mark Victor Hansen Pub. Co., 1989.

xxxviii Alexander, Scott. Rhinoceros Success: the Secret to Charging Full Speed toward Every Opportunity. Ramsey, 2011.

xxxix Proctor B. Art of Living [Internet]. TarcherPerigee; 2015. 240 p. Available from: https://www.goodreads.com/book/show/25310606-the-art-of-living

xl Borreli, Lizette. "Why Using Pen And Paper, Not Laptops, Boosts Memory: Writing Notes Helps Recall Concepts, Ability To Understand." Medical Daily, 7 Feb. 2014, www.medicaldaily.com/why-using-pen-and-paper-not-laptops-boosts-memory-writing-notes-helps-recall-concepts-ability-268770.

xli Nightingale, Earl. Lead the Field, Nightingale-Conant Corporation; 1986.

xlii Nightingale, Earl. Lead the Field, Nightingale-Conant Corporation; 1986.

xliii Hansen, Mark Victor., et al. Future Diary. Mark Victor Hansen Pub. Co., 1989.

xliv Shanley, J. P., Hanks, T., Ryan, M., & Bridges, L. (2002). Joe Versus the Volcano. Widescreen. Burbank, CA: Warner Home Video.

Made in the USA
Middletown, DE
24 December 2019